Snow Goose

Global Thanksgiving

GLOBAL PEACE -- HOW THE DREAM WILL

COME TRUE WITH GRANDMOTHER LOVE

Snow Goose

Global Thanksgiving

VICTOR VILLASEÑOR

SNOW GOOSE PUBLICATIONS

ACKNOWLEDGEMENT

First of all, I'd like to thank the forty-two people that Snow Goosed with us last year to Spain. I'd like to also thank Barbara, Myra and Linda for coordinating the entire effort.

Snow Goose Publications
1759 Oceanside Boulevard
Oceanside, CA 92054

Cover design by Joanne Martinez
Original artwork by David C. Villaseñor
Photograph by Joe Lopez
Song of the Snow Geese by Phil Swann

Villaseñor, Victor Edmundo.

CREED

Come and take in hand the wise Snow Goose's wing and fly through the needle's eye, pass war and hate, and greed and fear, back into Paradise on earth--which was never lost--but has lay...long unused.

Three Snow Geese Flying East
By David Cuauhtemoc Villaseñor

DEDICATION

This book of SNOW GOOSE GLOBAL THANKS-GIVING is dedicated to my grandmother, Doña Margarita, who died two years before I was born. In fact, she died on the same day--the same hour--that I was born, which in the Mexican culture is Mother's Day, May 10th, at midnight. Thank you, *Abuelita*; you are my special angel. *Gracias*.

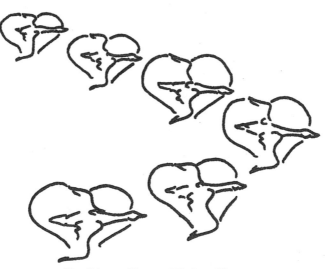

Six Snow Geese Flying East
By David Cuauhtemoc Villaseñor

TABLE OF CONTENTS

EXPLANATION

What is Snow Goose Global Thanksgiving? Well, the Snow Goose Global Thanksgiving is a vision that came to me in Portland, Oregon in the Fall of 1992 for worldwide peace and harmony on earth that will be further explained as we go along and get to know each other better.

So, for me, this is not a highly-polished, well-thought-out book like my regular writing, but a ''spontaneous rap session'' with God as I wrestled with our ''modern-day'' dilemma for worldwide peace and/or worldwide destruction.

So, there you have it. Thank you. *Gracias*. Hope this ''rap'' speaks to you as clearly and wonderfully as it spoke to me. *Con Dios*. Go with God, my friend, or may you walk in beauty, as the Navajos and Paiutes say.

Seven Snow Geese Flying East
By David Cuauhtemoc Villaseñor

PURPOSE

The purpose of The Snow Goose Global Thanksgiving is to inspire unconditional love, where all hearts open and all wines flow; a one-day-a-year event when all the people of the world can put aside their anger, hatred, prejudice, disappointments, for just three hours and totally concentrate all of their energies to the commitment of worldwide Thanksgiving for all of the "good" things we have, forgetting all the "bad" things and, also, give real heart-felt forgiveness for all the wrongs done on earth in thought or action, personal or institutional. A one-day-a-year event where we, the people, strip down spiritually naked within our own belief system and truly forgive ourselves down deep inside and all others and promote worldwide love, respect, tolerance and acceptance of all human beings--culturally, religiously, politically, sexually and, of course, dreamwise. For we are what we dream, and now is the time in human history to dream of worldwide peace and harmony between all God's children for the next 5,000 years.

Nine Snow Geese Flying East
By David Cuauhtemoc Villaseñor

CAN WE DO IT?

Yes, of course, we can. We can make this shared dream of Snow Goose Global Thanksgiving become a reality, and we can do it within ten to twenty years all over the world...we can if we want to, if we <u>really</u> want to.

You see, when I was a little boy and we lived on the ranch in Oceanside, California, I remember that we'd have a job to do and the best way to get that job done was to make it into an adventure...like cleaning up the old plum tree. When the season was over, there would be all these rotting plums on the ground, smelling badly and attracting flies and bugs all over the place. The plum tree was right outside my mother's kitchen window, and she wanted the place cleaned up so that she could open her window and get some fresh air and not have all these flies and hairy bugs coming inside and bothering her.

Well, I didn't want to end up doing the job all alone. That's no fun. Especially not in the summer. And, also, it was a dirty job. All the plums were rotten and slimy and smelly, so what I'd do was call my little sisters and all these cousins and nieces and nephews together and I'd explain the situation to them and then, with a big smile, I'd say, "I bet none of you can hit me or that trash can over there with any of these dirty old slimy plums!"

Well, I'll tell you, they'd get this gleam in their eye and instantly it was like I'd given them a free ticket to the Christmas spirit of giving, because they'd start picking up all those rotten, slimy plums and throwing them at me as fast as they could. Cleaning up that old plum tree would become the greatest adventure in all the world, and I'd be dodging and running and trying to catch all the plums they threw at me with that big trash can. In no time, my little sisters and cousins and nieces and nephews would have that old plum tree completely cleaned up. And they didn't care how dirty and slimy the job was. In fact, the slimier and dirtier, the better, because it was fun!

And fun, real, honest-to-goodness fun, can take us to places where reason doesn't dare go! How else do you think they ever got all those kids back in the Old West to leave the comfort of the three good meals that they had at home and become cowboys, riding at the hind-end of a herd of filthy, smelly cattle, eating tons of dust all day long? It was a time to be wild and free and there was challenge for them every day, every moment. It was fun!

So let's be children again. Let's return to that magic time before we started school, to that magic time before we started thinking linearly and we still believed in Santa Claus and we could make believe that cleaning up the old plum tree was fun. That's all we've got to do, challenge that lonely, lost adult inside each of us, and become cowboys and cowgirls again and ride herd on the ''old plum tree of life'' and drive us all back home into a world of peace and harmony for all humankind! And yes, with our vision, it will become a reality all over the globe in a very short time. All we have to do is WANT to do it and MAKE it fun, make it into the last new frontier on earth, the greatest challenge in all the world and, believe me, people will go far for fun and high adventure.

Remember, where reason DARE NOT GO!

* * *

Why do you think that war has been around for so long? Why do you think some of the best and brightest young, innocent minds have always been drawn to war like bears to honey? Because all these years, war has been promoted by the greedy and powerful to be the biggest, most fun adventure in all the world. War has always encouraged us not to have to face our own personal problems or shortcomings but, instead, we're always told that those people ''over there'' are our enemy, are the <u>real</u> source to all our aches and pains. We also get to play with all the latest and biggest toys, are given great, free uniforms, plenty to eat, and lead to believe that we're heroes--knights in shining armor--and we'll get the girl at the end of the battle, to boot! What boy or red-blooded man could resist? Suddenly, his life had meaning and purpose.

But now war is out of date. Television has completely ruined it by exposing it as the greedy, power-hungry game that it really is, run by insecure, frightened, old impotent men. Television has, also, saturated us with so much violence every single night--through the news and melodramas--that we've all become war-hardened veterans, whether we've been in actual combat or not. And then, all these gangs of kids with their drive-by shootings have also, thank God, brought home the message to us loud and clear that the wars of tomorrow are not going to be fought across that deep ocean or over that far mountain, but right here at home in our very own backyards unless, of course, we change our ways.

So, to answer the question: yes, one million times yes, worldwide peace and harmony on earth between all of God's children isn't only possible but, through our vision, inevitable. For the future has arrived; in fact, it's here already, right now, today, and the new game on the planet is called HARMONIC SURVIVAL. None of us--no matter how rich or powerful or how removed from the slums of war and hunger we might think we are--are going to survive the global disaster that we're already well into, if we don't change our ways...and

PRONTO!

So, yes, come join us and let us return to those days of magic when we all still believed in Santa Claus and let us ride herd on the old plum tree of life and, believe-you-me, world-wide peace and harmony between all God's children is in the bag! Because I don't care how slimy or dirty or rotten our life has become, or how destructive and terrible the world looks to you, we can clean it all up in no time at all, if we just keep loose and happy AND HAVE FUN! LOTS AND LOTS OF FUN!!! Right now! Today!

Ninety Snow Geese Flying East
By David Cuauhtemoc Villaseñor

IS THIS GOING TO COST ME ANY MONEY?

No. This isn't going to cost you one single dime. All you've got to do, to help pull off this miracle of miracles, is simply open up your heart this upcoming Thanksgiving to all the goodness that's already here inside of you; relax, enjoy yourself, and take it easy.

You see, the whole secret to happiness on earth and goodwill among all humankind is to realize that all happiness and well-being truly begins at home, here inside each and every one of us. Because if we're miserable, then the whole world looks miserable, too. And no matter how much we'd like to help the world we are going to fail and screw it up some more if we haven't put it together for ourselves, personally, *numero uno*.

You see, the world is going to survive with us or without us; so the key for the success of any global issue is that we've got to first be good and kind to ourselves; like each and every one of us needs to get plenty of good sleep and rest the night before Thanksgiving. And then you get up late on Thanksgiving day and just relax some more, and stretch and yawn like a lazy, fat cat. No big plans for golf or bicycling or getting in shape or saving the world or paying off all those bills or mortgages we owe, or doing any of those other things that we've been waiting to do for weeks, or months, or years. No, admit it down deep inside: this is a day to hang out with our loved ones, do nothing, and pig out! Yes, a day to be lazy and have no guilt whatsoever doing it.

In fact, pretend like this is your official job for the day, to be absolutely lazy and wonderful to yourself, really wonderful, and then to your loved ones. And so turn off that damn TV and don't answer the phone and don't read those crappy, "bad news" newspapers with all their negative crap. No, just relax and be a happy, lazy, summertime kid again, and make this into your very own special day, for you and your loved ones. And, also, don't make a big, fancy, expensive deal out of the dinner, either. Enjoy the magic of being an under-achiever for the day, a great glorious under-achiever, and just do one-fourth of what you'd normally do on Thanksgiving. In fact, what my family and I do at home is just lay around in bed, and whenever someone happens to come by we just say, "Take off your shoes and get in bed with us and help us do nothing!" Boy, you should see the smiles that come to their faces as they rip off their shoes and pile in with us and we chew the fat, talking about nothing important, and let the house be a mess--the messier the better, in fact. Hell, houses need a day of rest, too.

Okay, that's it. You've done it. And it didn't cost you

a single dime. Because you see, the first step, the very first step in bringing peace and harmony to all the world for the next 5,000 years isn't to use money as a tool, but to bring peace and harmony to yourself. That's what each and every one of us needs to do, needs to realize and truly understand...that all TRUTH, all REALITY really begins here inside each of us within our own heart and soul. Thank God!

So, now, feeling wonderful, we go to the table to PIG OUT where all hearts open and all wines flow! But before we pig out, let's just take one more moment and hold hands around the table and take a good, long look at each other and all of the food and smell it, really smell it, get into the smell and visual beauty of the feast that's before you and give thanks, thanks that you're alive, thanks that you're hungry, thanks to the people who prepared the food, and now fill your chest with love and pass this love around the table with your right hand; receiving this circle of love with your left. Realize now that we are, indeed, all God's children all over the globe and then send these good feelings of love out to the rest of the world, saying, "Thank You, God; thank You, God; thank You for this wonderful earth and food we are about to enjoy," and now sit down to eat and be happy, and laugh and have your meal with very little formality--just like the original Pilgrims and Indians did--two very different cultures who came together to share food with mutual respect and good-will.

That's it! We're done! Or, as the Navajos say, ''We finish in beauty!'' YES! ''WE FINISH IN BEAUTY!''

Three Hundred Snow Geese Flying East

By David Cuauhtemoc Villaseñor

WHY THE SNOW GOOSE?

This question is my favorite. You see, this entire concept of Snow Goose Global Thanksgiving came to me in a vision in the Fall of 1992, when I flew into Portland, Oregon on the promotional tour for my book *Rain Of Gold*. *Rain Of Gold* is the story of my parents who came from Mexico to the United States. The real heroes of the story are my two grandmothers, two *gran mujeres*, who were able to survive war, death and starvation because they never lost their faith in the infinite goodness of life.

Anyway, I'd been on tour for several weeks and I was tired, exhausted, completely drained. When I arrived in Portland, I was to do several high schools, some television and radio, and then speak at the Conant-Conant Bookstore, whose owners I'd met in L.A.

That evening, over a hundred and twenty people were crowded into the bookstore for my talk. Most of the audience was White-Anglo looking but there were, also, quite a few Latinos and local Indians. I began my talk by saying how poorly I'd done at school, flunked the third grade and encountered a lot of racism, but then how I'd finally gone to Mexico at the age of nineteen to stay with relatives and how I'd "discovered" myself by physically seeing and hearing and breathing my culture, then how books and education were able to save me, or I'm sure that I'd be in prison today for mass-murder--I'd had so much rage and hate inside of me.

I spoke with all my heart and soul and told my truth, wherever the cards might fall, and I explained that each and every one of us--and I didn't care if we were Black or White or Brown or Orange or Purple or had been raped or beaten or enslaved or born rich or poor or good-looking--we all had to come to terms with our own rage and hatred, with that loneliness and confusion that was gnawing inside each one of us, or we were lost. Then I further explained that we each had to get over the habit that we, humans, had of always blaming others for all our own problems and, instead, realize that each one of us had to rebuild ourselves into our own best hero, no matter what crap life has thrown at us. Because, if we didn't, then the only other alternative was to be all dead inside and live our whole life here on earth as a bitter, lost, angry, wimpy ass-whiner who was forever bitching and complaining and blaming others, including God, Himself, for his or her problems.

And I then told my audience that I knew what I was talking about, because I'd been there, I'd really been there, blaming the whole world for my problems for a long time, and so I could speak from personal experience of the deepest, meanest hatred! I began to cry, and half of the people started crying, too.

Then, in the back of the audience, a big, powerful, handsome Indian stood up and said, "Okay, you gave us a good personal rap, but now what are you going to do about Columbus?" The whole room quieted down. "The media is telling us that this is the year to celebrate the 500th anniversary of Columbus' discovery of the New World and my people and I are saying--just as your own life and book show--that this wasn't a discovery, but an INVASION!" he shouted. "A MASSACRE of all the native inhabitants and a RAPE of all our natural resources!"

The entire room was silent. He was a tall, imposing figure. And I didn't know what to say. I swallowed. "I don't know," I said.

"Well, you got to do something," he said. "You speak about God and truth and each of us finding ourselves. Well, then, you can't just back off now and let this misleading crap that the news media is feeding us go down, brother!"

I took a couple of deep breaths. I really didn't know what to say. And then another tall, big-faced Indian also stood up along with his smaller, shorter Mexican wife and he was crying so much that he couldn't speak. His wife finally spoke for him. "My husband has read your book," she said to me. "And he wants you to know that he's never read a book in the

White Man's language that has spoken to him before.''

    ''My heart!'' shouted the big-faced Indian. ''Your book spoke to my heart!'' And he placed both of his huge, dark brown, meaty hands on his chest and stood there, looking at me with so much love, offering me his heart. I was moved to the root of my being, and I could see that he wanted to say more, but he couldn't. His wife placed her small brown hand on his shoulder and his whole body began to jerk as he cried and cried, showing so much naked love for me and my book right there in front of everyone. Some people became nervous and wanted to leave; they weren't used to such openness of heart. But others loved it and began crying, too. The whole room became a holy place.

    ''My husband also wants you to know,'' his wife continued, ''that your grandmother is his grandmother, and that--that--'' She began to cry, too. ''--that we're all brothers and sisters, all of us all over the earth, coming from the same grandmothers, the same GRANDMOTHER LOVE of the earth itself!''

    I began to cry, too. For she'd spoken the truth. This was exactly what my book was all about, ''GRANDMOTHER LOVE'' from the ''GRANDMOTHER EARTH'', oh, yes, yes, a very special love, indeed. And now, here, I faced this other large dark brown Indian, looking like a piece of the earth itself, and I could feel his love too, even though it was covered up with so much hate and anger, just as I'd been for so many years.

"Look," I finally said, "the truth is that I just don't know what to say or do about Columbus. You see, I've never given Columbus that much thought." I spoke each word very carefully. I truly hated disappointing any of these people, who were being so open. But what could I do? I had to speak my own, personal truth. "And about this 500-year celebration, well, I really hadn't given it any importance, either." I shrugged. "Sorry. But for me, this whole Columbus thing is just a media ploy, because they're always so desperate to create news that I don't doubt that sometimes they're even tempted to go out and start their own war or disaster, just so they'll have something to show on the eleven o'clock news."

People laughed as I'd hoped that they would, but the big, handsome Indian didn't and yelled, "Exactly! And that's why you got to do something or the media will continue ruling our world with its sensationalism, selected coverage, and distorted truths!

"You're an important person!" he shouted even louder, staring straight at me, his eyes burning with passion. "The media listens to you, so you have to say something or do something! It's not right! These last 500 years have completely destroyed my people! And the earth, too! Columbus cannot be allowed to go down in history as a hero! He was not a good man! He came with a greedy, ugly heart, looking for quick profits! And the whole European influence followed his example and IS STILL FOLLOWING IT TODAY!''

A lot of people applauded him, cheering wildly, but others, I could see, were squirming in their seats. I took several deep breaths. I could feel chills going up and down my spine. I'd been hearing stuff like this from coast to coast for the last few weeks, but never with this intensity. My God, my heart was pounding so fast that it wanted to go and hide. I continued breathing, trying to quiet down my frightened heart. Then, finally, I spoke.

''Look,'' I said, ''I see what you're saying, *amigo*, but truthfully, I don't know what to tell you, much less what to do. Do you, do you have any suggestions on what should be done?''

''Yes!'' he said quickly, as if this was what he'd had on his mind all along. ''I want the TRUTH to be known! I want the media to not twist the FACTS around this time! I, I--'' He glanced up at the ceiling; he was on the verge of tears, and he raised his arms to the heavens. ''--we, we need--my people and me--need our skies returned to us!'' he said with power. Then, not knowing what else to say, he looked directly into my eyes with such desperate longing. "Mr. Villaseñor, get 'em...to give us back...our sky!" he said, and he started crying.

This time it was me who wanted to leave the room. I just didn't know how to handle such naked honesty. But I held. And I breathed deeply, deeply, relaxing down inside my center. "Okay, I see what you mean," I said, still breathing, still holding. "I understand. I really do. For, without our sky, we, we, a people, have no hope. We, a people, can't pray; 'cause we're lost. We are lost."

"YES," he shouted. "Exactly! You said it perfect! You do understand! WE ARE LOST!!!"

"Okay, *amigo*," I said, finally catching my breath and drying my eyes, "I'll tell you what I'll do...tonight, TO-NIGHT!" I screamed. "I'll, I'll...think about it. I'll think real hard about it, but...you must understand that my book is about my own family, and I'm only knowledgeable about what I personally know, so I can't promise you anything."

He was calming down now. I could see that our interaction, that speaking with our open hearts was calming us both down. "All right," he said, "but will you think about it with all the power that you used to write your book *Rain Of Gold*? I haven't read it yet," he added. "But my people are talking about it. It's supposed to be a great book. And it came out in 1992, the year of this so-called 'discovery', so you got to come up with something and," he breathed, "important!"

I wished my heart was braver, but it wasn't. And once more it took off running fast and wanting to hide. "Look," I said again, "I really can't promise you anything, much less something important, but I will think real hard about it tonight. In fact, I'll tell you what," I breathed a couple more times. I was getting a headache, this was so intense. "I'll even ask my grandmother, my spiritual guide, who was also Indian, to come to me tonight and help me. How about that?"

People started applauding, and the big, powerful, handsome Indian now came up through the crowd, smiling a big smile, and we hugged in a big *abrazo*. Now everyone starting cheering--White, Brown, Black, Yellow, Orange, Purple, whoever--and it was wonderful. My heart came back from hiding.

"Thank you for pushing me," I said to the big Indian. "I'm tired, really exhausted, but who knows?" I added. "We can always go a little farther."

"I'll be with you tonight," he said, kissing me. "And I'll ask my own grandmother to come and help you, too. She's been gone for years but she's still in good with all the local spirits."

"Good," I said, "I'll need her help. I'll need all the

help that I can get. Send all the spirits along, please. I'd be honored."

"It is done," he said, "finished in beauty." And he touched his chest, taking his heart and handing it to me, then he kissed me again, and now everybody was getting in line to embrace me, too.

One of the people was a nice-looking blondish man in his forties who gave me a big *abrazo* and whispered, "I'll be looking forward to what you come up with tonight, too. Columbus also did some good, you know. And remember, it took a lot guts to cross that ocean."

"Thank you," I said. "I appreciate your reminding me of that other side of the coin."

"Say 'hi' to your grandmother, Doña Margarita, for me tonight," he added, grinning. "I'm using *Rain Of Gold* in my classroom. Your grandmother reminds me of my own Irish grandmother. We've all been wronged, you know. Not just the Indians or the Blacks. Your book shows that, too."

"Thanks," I said again, and the people kept coming and coming to me, and I'm sure that I gave well over a hundred *abrazos* and signed over eighty books. And it had been going like this for me every day for well over three weeks now. All across the nation, but especially in the southwest, *Rain Of Gold* was becoming more than just a book; it was becoming an event; it was moving people's hearts and touching their very souls. (Like one woman from San Antonio, Texas who said that my grandmother was her grandmother, too, and she was German.)

Why, my book *Rain Of Gold* was reaching everyone and to think, my God, I'd almost quit writing it three different times. All those years of writing and doubting and wondering if I'd ever finish the book or get it published had paid off higher than my highest dreams. Oh, I felt blessed. So, who knew? Maybe I would come up with something important tonight, if I just relaxed and entrusted the universe to continue helping me.

I took a deep breath; boy, I was tired, exhausted, dropping.

* * *

And so that night after closing up the bookstore with the two owners and their two children, I walked down the street back to my hotel. I was sleep-walking, I was so exhausted. I'd been living on less than three or four hours of sleep for weeks now. I passed through the lobby of the peaceful old hotel where I was staying and went up to my room, washed up, stretched, did some deep breathing, asked the Almighty for rest and guidance, and then went to sleep, saying goodnight to my two grandmothers and my father, who'd recently passed away.

I was sound asleep when I first heard some laughter, like the far-away sounds of children playing on a playground. I continued sleeping, loving the sounds of the happy, playing youngsters, when I suddenly saw this gorgeous blue sky and some mountains in the distance and a bunch of little fat white clouds behind the mountains. I could hear that the sounds of the happy, laughing, screeching children came from above these distant clouds. Oh, these little kids were really having the time of the their lives.

Rolling over, I continued to sleep, truly enjoying the sound of the happy children and seeing the gorgeous blue sky, a sky so clear and beautiful that it just renewed my faith in the basic goodness of life. Then suddenly, from above the bunch of little fat clouds, I saw some beautiful white snow geese come flying toward me. They were large and white and truly beautiful as they came swimming toward me on their great white wings--wings so glorious against the background of the bright blue sky. They were squawking and screeching as they came over the rugged, green mountain range--happy, triumphant in all their natural glory. Then I realized that these snow geese--these great white birds--were, indeed, the children, the playground of happy children that I'd been hearing.

I lay there in bed, eyes wide open in complete wonderment. Then I felt myself being lifted up, up, up...and oh, my God, I was no longer in my room! I was flying, I was flying up above the good earth, and I could now see the snow geese so clearly, in such detail--each feather, each beak, each eye, each movement of individual head--as we now came flying together over these rugged pine-covered mountains.

Oh, it felt so good flying with these geese, with this playground of happy, screeching children just a couple of hundred yards up above the earth. And we were now approaching a luscious green meadow down below, and I just knew that this meadow did, in fact, really exist somewhere upon the earth because I could see it with such clarity and realistic detail. Why, this was no dream! No, this was really happening! I really was flying over the earth with a herd of happy snow geese children, squawking and screeching and laughing.

I glanced around. It was just before daybreak, and the whole eastern sky was painted in colors of soft pink and warm red and bright orange. And the huge flock of snow geese and I were now dropping down off the rugged mountain as we came over the luscious green meadow. I could see that the females and young flew in the center, and I could see that they were leading, directing, giving balance and tone to the flock with their loud squawking, talking, screeching. And I could also see that the bigger, strong males flew on the outside, cutting the wind for the flock and assisting with their power.

The flock passed over the valley, circling lower and lower, and they filled the heavens with their sounds of joy. Then I suddenly saw three big, strong males drop quickly out of the flock and go into the mist that covered the valley floor. I watched in wonderment as the three big males disappeared into the silvery mist, like big ghostly-white forms, chests huge and great white wings flapping, swimming in the early morning light--so brave, so sure, so confident, and then, suddenly, as I watched I understood that these big, strong males were going to check things out before committing the main of the flock, that these three big males were going down into the mist and they were prepared to die, to fight off men and wolves alike before allowing the main of the flock of females and young to expose themselves to any possible danger.

I watched, I watched in awe, in complete wonderment as the three big males disappeared like ghostly-white forms into the silvery mist, and I was stunned by of their absolute knowledge of who they were and what they were doing. Why, these three big white-winged males had dropped down into the mist with such power, with such joy, with such confidence, feeling perfectly at home in giving up their lives with unconditional love so that the main of the flock of women and children could survive.

I began to cry, I was so moved. Why, these geese, this tribe of ghostly-white birds truly knew how to live. For each of these great white birds knew who they were. The children and females knew that their place was to lead the flock by being happy and all-in-tune and these great, huge males knew that their place was to drop out of the flock into the silvery mist of the unknown with a Christ-like elegance of love and faith and--oh, it was so beautiful! So, so, so beautiful and I was weeping like a baby--I was so happy, and suddenly I was back in my room, and I had this hunger, this thirst to have this same absolute knowledge for my own male-human-self that these brave male snow geese had for themselves as they'd dropped out of the flock, prepared to die, to die, to give their lives with unconditional love, so that the main of the flock could survive!

Oh, I was so happy! And I wiped my eyes and curled back up and tried to go to sleep again, but then I began to flash on the prior evening and on that big, powerful Indian, who'd demanded that I come up with something important, and I tried to understand what was being said to me by this vision of ghostly-white birds who were still flying all around me in the silvery early morning mist inside of my mind's eye, and then I saw it; I saw it so clearly. Why, my grandmother, Doña Margarita, was telling me that we, human beings, were, indeed, THESE SNOW GEESE. Yes, we really were THESE SNOW GEESE, if only we relaxed and opened up our soul to the absolute knowledge of our infinite love for one another. For we, too, were a flock, a tribe of women and children and men just like THESE SNOW GEESE.

I sat up, and my mind began to reel in flashes of rapid pictures, and once more, I saw the Snow Geese coming over the mountain and approaching the luscious green meadow and I suddenly knew everything. Why, my grandmother was telling me that the time in human history had come for us to accept our absolute SNOW GOOSE LOVE for one another. That the last 5,000 years of human history had only been that tiny, little, ''approach time'' that I'd just seen when those three big white males had dropped out of the herd and taken the lead into the early morning mist. And that these last 5,000 years of male leadership as we, all humankind, had dropped out of the sky into the silvery mist that covered the luscious green earth were now ''done'', ''finished'', ''completed in beauty'', and now it was that time in human history for the women and children to once more resume our leadership.

Wow! My heart was pounding. I was stunned, I was

shocked with the clarity of what my mind was thinking, and
I didn't move a single muscle. No, I just lay there in bed with
my eyes wide open, not wanting to miss a single thought, a
single word, a single picture frame that was being spoon-fed
to me by my grandmother. And THESE SNOW GEESE OF
OURSELVES kept flying about inside of my mind's eye and
now all of history made so much sense to me. Why, no wonder
that the last 5,000 years had been so full of aggression and war
and world domination. It had all been done within the spirit
of those Three Big Male Snow Geese dropping out of the flock
and going down to check things out on the earth. But now that
stage of our development was over, because males were just
too strong, too powerful to lead for very long, or they'd
automatically set a pace that was too hard, too fast for the main
of the tribe and it would drive the women and children into
panic and fear and mass-confusion. Only the women and
children could set a pace that was softer, slower, and more
open to the possibilities of peace and harmony and happiness
and long-range well-being.

A great peace came over me. And suddenly all of our
past human history seemed okay to me. In fact, I could now
see that it had all been absolutely necessary so we could get to
where we now stood. And then I saw even further and further
and I came to realize that Columbus had, indeed, been a good

man, a wonderful man, for he'd sailed into uncharted waters. And yes, and he'd sailed with three tiny ships bobbing up and down in the great dark sea looking like lost little white birds with their tall wind-filled sails. Oh, Columbus truly was a Big Snow Goose Hero and so was that big, handsome Indian who'd pushed me so hard last night. He, too, was another Big Snow Goose Hero. For he was also right, these last 500 years had been full of greed and rape and destruction of all kinds and it had to stop!

Tears came to my eyes. My God, we'd all gone through so much suffering, so much terrible pain in the last five centuries; especially in the last 100 years. Why, it almost seemed as if the whole last 5,000 years of human experience had all been aimed to climax in the last 100 years and now was the time to...

I stopped. My mind exploded. I just couldn't handle the on-rush of picture-thoughts that I was receiving. And the Snow Geese now went into a spin, a whirling spiral of motion, gaining infinite speed, and then, and then I caught a glimpse, and then another glimpse, and I now saw that yes, absolutely yes, these last 5,000 years hadn't just been necessary, but that they were, indeed, wonderful, absolutely glorious, for they had given us, Our Human Tribe Of Snow Geese the confidence, the knowledge to come to the realization that yes, we could destroy the whole human world if we wished, or we could clean up the whole human world if we so chose. Oh, yes, yes, yes! This was our power, our gift, and, and, either way, God would still love us and the world, the universe would go on with us or without us, and it was all okay.

* * *

I must have passed out. Because I don't remember what came next. I guess my human mind just couldn't conceive what I'd received. Not in words. Not in thoughts. Not with all I'd been trained to think about God and Hell and Judgment Day, but then, here I was awake again, and there it still stood: simply, God loved us, no matter what.

A great, great peace came over me, and I breathed and breathed and I suddenly saw, realized, understood that yes, it really was absolutely up to us to destroy our world or to clean up our world if we choose; that this was our power, this was our gift given to us by the Creator when we'd choose to go out of The Garden on our own, choosing free-will over our perfect harmony with God.

I breathed, I breathed, I breathed. And I truly now saw that this was what every child did when they left the nest, too; they developed the capacity of choice. And so, yes, after 5,000 years of struggle and pain, we, as a people, now stood on the threshold of almighty choice; the same choice that God, in His infinite wisdom, bestowed upon each and every planetary system when He saw that they were now ready to EXPLODE into their next stage. And so, yes, now we were ready and it really was in us to destroy ourselves, returning to darkness, or to blossom and return OURSELVES to GOD, in all OUR OWN NEWLY-FOUND GLORY AND WONDERMENT OF THE LAST 5,000 YEARS!!!

I breathed, I breathed deeply, deeply, relaxing down deep inside of myself. And I breathed and breathed and breathed and the quiet peace inside of me grew and I knew that this was wonderful. Why, this was truly our great gift of free-will that I'd been taught so much about by the nuns when I'd been a little boy. This was our present, our gift given to us by the Almighty, which truly made us in His Own Image, and so this was, indeed, beautiful; for it really was all entirely up to us what we decided to do.

Our bombs, our wars, our TVs, our highrises, our airplanes, our computers, our fax machines, all these were but mere toys, given to us in order to satisfy our male ego, and so now that we'd accomplished all this, we could relax and make Our Decision; and, either, allow ourselves to blossom into the female side of our own natural wonderfulness, so that, with

our female intuition, we could now space-travel within ourselves a zillion times faster than the speed of light and shoot
beyond all thinking and reason and come to know, to truly
KNOW the truth which is that WE ARE ALL WONDERFUL,
that we are all really children of God; that we are all, in fact,
angels--each and every one of us--we are angels; we are The
Messengers Of The Light, The Snow Goose People, THE
SOURCE OF OUR OWN ENLIGHTENMENT...or, We
could go the opposite direction and destroy ourselves as we
were presently doing, and either way God would still love us!

I took another deep, deep breath, feeling for the first
time in all my life so thoroughly calm and happy and blessed.
Why, the clarity of this incredible information that I'd received felt so just right. God would still love us even if we
destroyed the whole human world; this was beautiful and yet
felt so strange.

I shook my head. "Grandmother," I said, "I don't get
it. It feels so good to know this. Really, so good down here
in my stomach, but up here in my head, I feel like, well, maybe
I should be, well, punished for having such an idea."

I heard laughter, wonderful laughter, and then I heard
my grandmother Doña Margarita say to me inside of my mind.
"Didn't God give us His Only Begotten Son to crucify? Does
not a mother still love her child even when he or she breaks her

best plate? Oh, yes, this thought you've been given makes perfect sense here inside every mother's heart. For remember, the universe is infinite and God has billions of earths like a mother has dozens of plates and love has no limits, *mi hijito*; love, in fact, only gives more love, so there can be no punishment.''

Hearing Grandmother's words, I immediately felt an even greater peace come over me. Why, yes, of course! Only by God giving us the reassurance of Everlasting Unconditional Love could we then love each other here on earth unconditionally, too.

Tears of joy came to my eyes and I breathed and I breathed, and all thoughts and feelings of Judgment Day and punishment left my soul forever, and yes, yes, yes, the Sky opened up and there was Heaven in all its glory and I now saw that any group or person who proclaimed damnation or a revengeful deity, missed the whole boat. They missed the whole boat or they were lost, and/or they were out of date, or misusing God's name to scare people so that they could then manipulate them as they pleased. And then I was flying. I was flying once again over the earth with all these squawking, screeching Snow Goose Children and I was so happy. So very happy, and all of the Earth was luscious green and the Sky was bright blue and ALL OF HUMAN HISTORY now seemed so "okay", so crystal clear, and really sensible. And the great peace continued to grow inside of me, to blossom, to give me this all-knowing feeling, this all-at-home-deep-inside-of-me feeling, and I was so happy, so very happy to know that God loved me no matter what.

I began to cry. I felt like ten thousand million years of human-tension had just been stripped away from me, and I now knew very clearly what was my own personal choice; for these beautiful White Birds had shown me the way. These wonderful, Glorious Angels Of Ourselves, had just taken me to the Other Side of the Great Beyond and had shown me a whole other way in which to view our total human experience in relationship to God's Infinite Love; another way in which all of us could truly see ourselves entirely different, for we had choice; we could choose to become The Tribe Of Our Own Bird People, or not. And so, yes, of course, I choose to LOVE MY GRANDMOTHER EARTH. I, a human male, choose to become more and more Christ-like like those three male Snow Geese who'd been willing to give their lives with unconditional love so that the main of the flock could survive. For truly it was in Us to be our own Best Heroes; for We were, indeed, a part of God, and God was Us, and We were God, and now was the time in human history for all of Us to accept this simple fact, and then make Our own private, personal choice.

For We had arrived; We, The Tribe Of The Bird People; We, The Wonderment Of Ourselves had finally arrived after 5,000 years of "approach time" and God loved Us, and We loved God, and now the choice was Ours, all OURS, to become His Blessed Children, treating each other with unconditional love, now that our collective male egos had been satisfied at last, thank God, or to destroy Ourselves. It was all Our choice. And I, for one, was choosing to accept the Angel of Myself, and give back the reins to the woman-part inside of me. For men, too, were included, you know. For all human beings were, indeed, both male and female, and now was the time for Us here on earth to relax and allow Ourselves to slip, to slide back into Our Own Great Female/Male Balance of Enlightenment, Fulfillment.

I breathed, I breathed, I breathed. I breathed, I breathed, I breathed. I breathed, I breathed, I breathed, I breathed. I breathed, I breathed, I breathed, I breathed, I breathed, feeling so, so, so, so, so, so, so Blessed. Oh, this gift, this vision that I'd just been gifted was so much greater, so infinitely larger than just about Columbus and his "invasion" and/or "discovery" of the New World. Why, this gift drove Us, all Humankind, back down deep into our very core, our very root, OUR VERY SOUL OF WHAT IT WAS TO BE HUMAN! And to be human, WITHOUT JUDGMENT,

WAS ABSOLUTELY WONDERFUL! THANK YOU, GOD! THANK YOU! And I ACCEPT!

* * *

I must've gone to sleep, because the next thing I knew I was waking up and stretching, yawning, and feeling so good and warm and really quiet. I glanced around and it was still dark. Then I remembered the Snow Geese and the vision I'd had, and I took a few deep breaths.

My God! Why, I'd found out that to be human was a zillion million times greater-reaching than I'd ever antici- pated. Why, God really had bestowed upon Us the POWER, the ABSOLUTE POWER to become Christ-like children if We so choose, to truly walk on water if We just relaxed and accepted Ourselves to the root of Our Own Wonderfulness. Why, our little messy predicament here on earth was easy to clean up! No more than a little old plum tree of a problem; no big deal for Us, this Wonderful Species Of Pure Wonderment, created in God's Own Image.

I stretched and yawned some more. Oh, I felt so Blessed, so Holy, so Good. Why, we were all Winners. Each and every one of Us. There were no losers, no ''them'' or ''they'' or ''enemy'' among Us.

Why, men were now free to be men! To drop out of the flock into the silvery morning mist of the unknown and die like heroes if they so chose. Why, it was now all right for me to be a healthy, horny male and like the rush of a motorcycle, the quickness of a fast horse, the rapids of a fast river, the craziness of a wild drunk, or the wonderful violence of a good-bloody boxing match or football game; and no woman had the right to "nag" me. Oh, this was beautiful! Absolutely beautiful! Men could be men; women could be women; children could be children, and no one group had the "right" to criticize or put judgment on the other's style or force "their's" on others. I liked it, I loved it; it made perfect sense.

Why, the whole world had just been turned inside out for me and handed to me on a GOLDEN PLATTER OF BRILLIANT ENLIGHTENMENT. And I, a man, a male, didn't have to really give up anything in order to join Our Future Female Wonderfulness! No, instead, I finally got to be what I'd always, secretly, wanted to be: a hero, a checker-outer-of-the-early-morning-silvery-mist, and we could still have a safe, good world for the main of the flock who needed a softer, kinder pace.

And once more I now saw those Three Snow Geese Heroes drop out of the flock. I saw them drop out and I could now enjoy them at even a deeper level, feeling even more

WONDERFUL than I'd felt the first time that I'd seen these three big, strong males drop down out of the flock and disappear into the early morning mist, willing to die, to die for their loved ones with such confidence, such Christ-like elegance for...the women and children were leading the main of the flock and our future was...safe.

Chills went up and down my spine--these Great White Birds truly knew how to live. For each completely accepted the other for who they were. And all my life I'd wished to be accepted by my family and children unconditionally for all my crazy, fearlessness, for all my *loco* bravery as I dropped into the unknown, the unmapped, the unreachable, the impossible.

*   *   *

So I glanced at my watch, saw it was half past three, and decided to go back to sleep. I'd truly enjoyed the ''Snow Goose Vision'' that my grandmother had given me, but now I was really tired and needed to go back to sleep, so I could catch another plane in the morning and continue on my book tour.

But then, to my utter surprise, I'd no more than turned over when I heard my grandmother yelling at me. No kidding. She was yelling and saying that we weren't done.

I sat up. Oh, my grandmother was going too far. "Look, Grandmother," I said, losing all patience, "it's fine for you who's dead and up in heaven to have all these great insights and to give some of them to me now and then so I can write about them, but I need my sleep now! So, please, no more! That's it! I'm going to sleep. Goodnight!"

And I turned over, hit my pillow a few times, and tried to go back to sleep, but no matter how much I tried, I couldn't. "Okay," I finally said, opening my eyes, "so what's your idea, Grandmother? Shoot; go on, I'm listening."

"Well," she said, "simply, the time has come, *mi hijito*, for God's love to be done. It's not enough anymore for people to know, it must be done, too."

I took a big breath. "But, Grandmother, what is it that you're asking me to do, exactly? My God, the world is already full of fanatics who are going around, shoving all these different beliefs down people's--"

"*Mi hijito*," she said with great patience, "simply invite our loved ones to come together like the happy, playful children of God that we are and turn our planet, our lives, back into Paradise On Earth and realize that we can do it by this upcoming Thanksgiving."

I was astonished. "Listen, Grandmother," I said, "it's one thing to have great insights into human nature, but it's a whole other ballpark to try and turn them into reality--and by Thanksgiving, good God!''

''Exactly,'' she said, ever so calmly, ''and with Our Good God's help, it will be done.''

I swallowed. I breathed a few times. ''Look, Grandmother,'' I said, ''Thanksgiving is only a few weeks away. I don't think you're being realistic."

She smiled. ''And how long did it take Our Lord God, the Creator, to make the world, *mi hijito*?''

''Hey, just wait,'' I said to her. ''You can't compare me to God and what He was able to accomplish in a week, Grandmother!''

''And why shouldn't I compare you to God?'' she said. ''Why, God is the absolute best in each of Us. Who else would you have me compare you to? Eh? You tell me? Why, I have always compared my children and my children's children to God, Himself, and...TO DO LESS IS AN OUTRAGE!'' she shouted with *gusto*.

I nodded. ''Okay, I see your point, Grandmother,'' I said. ''I'd just never quite seen it like that before. But, still, what is it that you're asking me to do exactly? Remember, I'm on a book tour, and I'm really tired, and this book tour is important to me and my family--I mean, our family.''

''And did I say that your book tour isn't important?

Did I suggest that you not continue doing your earthly responsibilities? Ah, did I?''

"Well, no, you didn't, *Abuelita*, but remember, I can't do everything. I'm still only a human being in an earthly body and I'm exhausted and I need to sleep sometime, you know.''

"Only a human being,'' she said. I swallowed. I could feel that she was pissed. "Why, to be a human being is glorious!'' she said. "To be a human being in an earthly body is to be the living, breathing tissue of God! To be a human being is to be without limits; for you are the anchor of the spiritual world; and together we are the Stars, the Heavens, the Beauty of Our Own Makings! Do you hear me?! We are God! And God is Us!''

My heart was running to hide, but it couldn't figure which way to go. "Yes, *Abuelita*, I hear you,'' I finally said. "I'm sorry. I take it back. Really!''

"Good,'' she said. "And about you being exhausted. Well, wasn't I exhausted and in the middle of a war, but I still had the presence of mind to push aside my exhaustion, and promise your father that we'd live and that I'd see him married and with children, and now here you are, his child, and so YOU WILL NOT BE EXHAUSTED!'' she screamed. "Do you understand? YOU WILL NOT BE EXHAUSTED!''

I took a deep breath. "Okay, okay,'' I said. "I won't

be exhausted.'' Good God, it was really hard arguing with Grandmother. Whatever I brought up, I was sure that she could bring up something a thousand times worse and still show me how she'd lived through it and triumphed. ''All right,'' I said. ''I'm not tired and as a human being I'm capable of moving mountains, but I still don't, well, quite understand what it is exactly that you want me to do. I got the 'vision' of the 'Snow Geese', that I understand, but it's not like I'm some famous TV figure, Grandmother, and can just go on the air and announce to the whole world this vision that you've given me. So, well, don't you think that maybe it's just best for me to get some sleep now and maybe some day write a book about all this and then let people read it and lead themselves into this new way of looking at things?'' I took a deep breath, hoping I could get her to back off. ''Look, Grandmother,'' I said, trying to bring the whole thing to a close, ''I'm just a writer; I'm not a world leader, or politician, or anything like that. Sorry.''

But as soon as this last sentence had left my mouth, I knew I'd made another big mistake. For the Power, the Presence that I now felt come off of Grandmother was so intense that my heart took off in fear. Oh, she was really pissed off again, and the whole room vibrated with her Power.

''Are you the flesh of my flesh?'' she asked.

"Well, yes, I am," I said.

"Are you the spirit of my spirit?" she asked.

"Yes, I am," I said.

"THEN!" she shouted. "You will now rise up and come forward! For there are no great leaders of the world! There are no powerful, all-knowing *politicos*! There is only Us, the People, You and I, and this is Our Power, Our Strength, that We, The Meek, *La Gente Del Pueblo*, have inherited the earth from this day forth, and We are Our Own Best Leaders for WE KNOW OUR FLOCK! Do you hear me? We know our flock!

"Now get up, and start writing, since that is what you do, and my great, well-earned wisdom of the ages will come from me through you as you write."

"But, do you still mean for all this to happen by this Thanksgiving?" I asked. She didn't even bother answering me. "Okay, okay," I said, getting out of bed. "I'll start writing, but I have no idea where to begin and what it's going to be...oh, I see a children's book. But a children's book for adults. Oh, a book that adults buy and read WITH their kids, so that they can turn off the TV and visit together as a family.

"Oh, I see, I get it, I'm cooking. But I still can't really see how all this Snow Goose business and the American celebration of Thanksgiving are going to tie in with Columbus, Grandmother. And, besides, I think that Thanksgiving and Columbus happened a couple of hundred years apart, too.''

I was suddenly struck with a flash of such power that I shut the hell up. I turned off my word-thinking mouth, took a few more deep breaths, and my all-heart-knowing soul opened up, and then, there it was, and I saw it all so crystal clear, and now it all made perfect sense.

Why, Grandmother was absolutely a genius! Yes, of course, Thanksgiving had everything to do with Columbus. Why, Thanksgiving had come to be, directly BECAUSE of Columbus. Thanksgiving, in fact, was the only celebration in all the Americas--that I knew of--that had to do with the European invasion where the invaders had actually had a meal in peace and harmony with the natives, and neither was made the lesser for it. Why, the Pilgrims and Indians had actually shared bread and real friendship together with mutual respect. Why, it was the only celebration in the New World that I knew of that still continued to exist to this very day on a yearly basis that gave wholesome well-being to the meeting of the European people and the American natives. And, also, it showed that the new arrivals had been desperate, and that it was the Indians--the native people--who'd showed them how to plant and where to fish and hunt, and how to survive the harsh winters.

This was WONDERFUL! Thanksgiving was a celebration through which we could bring out the best of the Europeans, the best of the Indians, and sidestep all this anger and hatred that people were feeling toward Columbus and help us all to BLOSSOM TOGETHER into a whole new level of ENLIGHTENMENT!

And sure, of course, it was said that things had gotten sour shortly after that memorable Thanksgiving when supposedly, a young Indian boy was killed by the Pilgrims because he and one of the Pilgrim's daughters had fallen madly in love. But, still, that didn't take away from the fact, that for one small, precious, golden moment, two very different cultures had put aside their differences--religiously, politically, sociologically--and they'd given thanks to the Mighty Creator in unison of spirit and heart and open soul!

Yes, oh, God, yes! This was it! Grandmother was absolutely right, this was the key to our entire worldwide march toward peace and harmony--Global Snow Goose Thanksgiving! Or, maybe better, The Snow Goose Global Thanksgiving, or maybe still better Thanksgiving Of The Global Snow Goose. I smiled. I grinned. I laughed. No matter what we called it, the concept was there, and it was a good concept, because we weren't going to have to reinvent the wheel from scratch. No, we were going to use a wonderful celebration that was already recognized by well over 200 million people, and it wasn't going to cost anyone a dime to participate. Why, they could do their part of this global celebration from the privacy of their own homes.

Families were going to get together all over the country anyway, and so this was just a little turn of the OLD LOVE SCREW and--BINGO! they'd be doing their part of our worldwide effort of Snow Goose Global Thanksgiving toward peace and harmony on earth for the next 5,000 years!

Oh, it was BEAUTIFUL! And now all we needed was a book, or a song, or a movie, or all three, and then, yes, maybe an actual physical location, too, so we could kick the event off. Why, yeah, we'd go to Spain. Yeah, Spain was where Columbus had come from so, yeah, I'd get a bunch of friends and relatives together and we'd go back to Spain and celebrate our first official Global Thanksgiving with the King of Spain, reversing the flow of the negative energy that Columbus had brought westward in the name of greed and profit and rigid religious order. Why, we'd fly eastward like Those Three Great White Snow Goose who'd dropped into the silvery mist to check things out and we'd land in Spain in peace and harmony and goodwill--forgiving Columbus for all his trespasses--and we'd see what happens to us. Yeah, we'd land in

Spain and put into motion goodwill among all humankind and we'd keep doing it every year for the next 34 years until we reached the year 2026.

I stopped and glanced at my grandmother. "But wait, why until the year 2026?" I asked.

"Because that's the end of the 52-cycle of--look, you don't need to know why right now," she said. "Just keep writing and listening and you'll catch on."

"Okay," I said, smiling. Oh, this was fun. And so I continued writing and listening, being completely open to my grandmother's presence, and then I saw us; all these people, women and children, men and teenagers, and we were all flying eastward on the wings of these Three Mighty Snow Geese, and then we were landing, landing, coming down into the silvery mist of Spain and all these cheering, happy people were there to greet us, and it was wonderful! Absolutely wonderful! The beginning of a whole new wild frontier of world peace! The biggest adventure on the entire planet! More exciting than war or reading TV or watching the newspapers!

"Why, Grandmother," I found myself saying, "I can see it now! I can really see it; I'll take out a whole page ad in the *L.A. Times* or *N.Y. Times* and invite everyone to put on their cowboy hats and cowgirl pants and come to Spain with us and ride herd on cleaning up the "old plum tree of life", and...WE ARE GOING TO DO IT THIS YEAR, RIGHT NOW! In just a few weeks from now! Yiiiieeeee-i-ooooo!"

Grandmother started laughing. I started laughing, too. "So what's so funny?" I asked.

"You," she said, "only moments ago you were too tired to even hear me out."

I grinned. "That was twenty thousand million years ago! SO COME ON, GIVE ME SOME MORE, *Abuelita*! Just keep throwing those old slimy, rotten plums at me! And I'll catch 'em all in this old trash can! Oh, this is FUN!"

"I'm proud of you, *mi hijito*," I heard her say. "We're all so very proud of you, and We want you to know that you are not alone; the Spirit Of The HOLY GHOST is already flying strong all over the globe and the moment you announce your quest, entire organizations of other Snow Goose People are going to come forth, and you will all grow and multiply beyond your wildest dreams; and Thanksgiving will, indeed, become a once-a-year event where all of The Bird People Of The Earth will come together to see each other and interact, sharing love and well-being and harvest the fruits of peace-making from all parts of the globe." She grinned. "So tell people to eat and be merry so that your wings will continue to grow, for now is the time for all human beings to be

STRONG! STRONG WITH LOVE! And inexhaustible! For we are WONDERFUL, and the earth is GOOD! And GOD LOVES US, no matter what!''

"Yes! Yes! I get it! But just wait; hold on,'' I said. "Do you mean that tens of thousands will be coming to Spain this year with us, Grandmother?''

"Well, maybe not this year,'' she said. "But in a very, very short time you will be so many that the flutter of your wings alone will change the winds of all humankind. People will be smiling and they won't know why. Strangers will speak to one another and they'll rejoice, for they speak from the heart. You see, *mi hijito*, the truth is that we have always been good people, very good people; it's just that we got lost for a little while, building things and telling each other the worst about ourselves.'' She shrugged. "But that's all over now. It's done. Finished. Gone.''

"I see, I see, and so now is the time for us to tell each other about the best in ourselves, eh?''

"Exactly. And people will come with power and energy and LOVE from all corners of the earth to rejoice! For they, too, have MEMORIES of Paradise and LONG to be WHOLE again!''

"But, my God,'' I said excitedly, "if that many people come to Spain with us this year, how will we feed them, or house them? And will I need to notify the authorities and get permits, or what?"

"Did Columbus notify the inhabitants of the *Mejico* that he was coming? Did Columbus get permits to bring all his people and doings to this part of the earth? Oh, no, *mi hijito*, you ask no questions nor tell any authorities; you simply invite all *la gente* of the world and they will come and feed themselves and every door of every home in all the earth will open and house them. For the earth is now ready for all of God's children all over the land to come forth with open hearts to become the Snow Geese that they, indeed, already are and have always been, and allow The Angel in each and every one of Us to rise up out of Our Souls, so Every Human Being can then see who has eyes to see, and every human being can then hear who has ears to hear, and they can open their hearts to the absolute knowledge that the time has come for the SKY OF OUR DREAMS, the SKY OF OUR LORD GOD'S LOVE to return to us, so that We, The Snow Geese People Of Ourselves, may now dream the dream of returning home; home to ourselves on wings of good tidings for all of us to hear and know that, yes, The Bird Tribe has arrived; The Bird Tribe Of The Angels Of Ourselves has ARRIVED IN ALL GOD'S GLORY!"

Oh, I was mesmerized. I took a few deep breaths, and

then I leaped up, yelling, shouting, screeching, jumping up and down and DANCING with wild happiness! Good God, I'd asked and I had received! I'd asked and I'd RECEIVED! I'd asked and I'd been GIVEN BEYOND MY WILDEST DREAMS! Why, I'd told that big, handsome Indian that I'd give it a try, even though I was dropping from exhaustion, and here now I was, jumping up and down and DANCING, knowing that the whole world was in our hands, in our hands, IN OUR HANDS and I was feeling this incredible surge of BOUNDLESS ENERGY AND CONFIDENCE!

Oh, I was EXPLODING! There wasn't a tired bone in all of my body. Finally, I stopped dancing, calmed down, and realized down deep inside of myself that I'd just witnessed a MIRACLE OF MIRACLES, here, inside my hotel room in Portland, Oregon of ASTONISHING PROPORTIONS!

I felt a Holy Presence come into me, and I began to shake, to vibrate and felt icy cold, and then to cry. I knelt down on the floor and gave thanks to the Almighty Creator, thanking The Great Spirit over and over again. And, instantly, the icy-cold-feeling left me and I felt this incredible warmth, this incredible BLISS come shooting into me, filling every cell of my entire being, and I now knew without a shadow of a doubt that I, too, had just come home; yes, indeed, I, personally, had finally returned HOME, HOME within me, myself, to my very own Human Snow Goose Bird Of Myself and I was now at peace, at peace, at peace, oh, yes, at peace.

And I began to chant, sounding like a playground of happy, playing children up in the bright blue sky of our dreams.

Six Hundred Snow Geese Flying East

Seven Hundred Snow Geese Flying East

Nine Hundred Snow Geese Flying East

Nine Thousand Snow Geese Flying East

Thirty Thousand Snow Geese Flying East

Sixty Thousand Snow Geese Flying East

Seventy Thousand Snow Geese Flying East

Ninety Thousand Snow Geese Flying East

By David Cuauhtemoc Villaseñor

HOW TO APPROACH PEOPLE

Well, I chanted for a while and then sat down and wrote for about three hours, and then I decided to get out on the street and stretch my legs and try out "my new-found" knowledge on a few people and see how it went. For I'd found out, by going through the school of hard-knocks, that it was one thing to know everything in the world all by yourself locked up in the safety of your home or room, drug or drink, but it was a whole other matter to take it out and test it on the people in the street. The streets were reality. That's where every person worth their salt had to go after their forty days in the desert. So here I was, walking up the street in front of my hotel, just after daybreak, when I happened to come upon a man on the corner. "Wonderful morning, isn't it?" I said. He was White and in his thirties.

"Well," he said, "it's still a little early for me."

"Just the way I like it!" I said with energy to spare. "By the way," I added, wondering how to best say this. But then, before I could think, it all just came pouring out of me. "I've just come up this morning with a wonderful idea for bringing peace and harmony throughout the world for the next 5,000 years, starting this upcoming Thanksgiving. So what's your first reaction to my statement? Honestly, your first reaction.''

"Well," he said, glancing me over, checking out my cowboy boots and western hat, "my first reaction is I need a cup of strong coffee." He smiled.

I could see that he was more than a little nervous. "Well, okay," I said. "So you need a strong cup of coffee. But what do you think of the idea?"

"Well," he said, straightening up, glancing around as if he wanted to get away from me, "I think that's a nice idea, but...well, it will never work. There will always be fighting and war on earth."

"Why? Because that's the way it's always been in the past?"

"Absolutely!" he said, beginning to wake up.

"Well, I say bull! Why, there's more peace on earth right now at this very moment than war all over the globe!"

"Hey, don't you read the papers?" he said quickly. "Ah, what's wrong with you? Don't you watch TV?" He was getting hot. "Didn't you see those riots that happened down in L.A.?"

"Well, okay, take the L.A. riots," I said. "Why, that was only a small portion of the people who were rioting."

"But that's not true!" he snapped excitedly. "I read the papers, I watch TV, I know history, and I can see that we're headed for disaster! There's violence going on everywhere!''

Hearing this, I got it, I now really understood what my grandmother had meant by saying that we'd gotten "lost" by telling each other about the worst of ourselves. "Well, friend, I say bull to all this, too! Hell, people who watch the newspapers and read TV are the most misinformed fools on the whole planet. Because they start thinking that that's reality when, in fact, reality is here, right now, between you and me. This is reality, friend. And I'm not beating the crap out of you, and you're not shooting and stabbing me, and so this is peace, friend. This is peace," I said, sticking out my hand. "Victor Villaseñor," I added. "A peacemaker."

Quickly, he looked at my out-stretched hand, but he didn't take it. "Look, I don't want to rain on your parade," he said, calming down, "but you have to admit that, maybe, you and I aren't fighting at this moment, but the rest of the world is pretty screwed up." He laughed.

"Bullshit on this one, too!" I said, taking back my hand and not liking his laughter. "Why, that's the most arrogant statement a human being can make, *amigo*. Because the truth is you don't really know anything about the rest of the world, except for the third-hand crap you read in papers and see on TV. I say to you that I've just toured the whole country, twenty-some cities, and on first-hand knowledge, I can tell you that the rest of the world, my friend, is just fine and dandy. And anyone who thinks it's screwed up is either too mentally lazy to think for themselves or should just take a good, long look in the mirror and realize that it's their own sick face that they're seeing.'' He started to leave. ''Hey, wait! Just hold on; please, let me finish! This is worldly important!'' He stopped. ''Listen,'' I said, ''this upcoming Thanksgiving is the beginning of peace and harmony for the whole world for the next 5,000 years, and Global Thanksgiving and global forgiveness is the key. You see, the world is okay, and it's always been okay. Sure, there are hard times here and there and some fighting going on, too, but this is the challenge of life, the challenge of living, not the fear of dying or thinking that we're on the brink of disaster!''

''Jesus,'' he said, turning back to see me, ''who are you?'' He shook his head and he took a couple of deep breaths. ''Do you honestly believe that we're okay with all the violence that's going on?'' he asked. ''My God, every day I get up, thinking this could be the end!''

''And, my friend,'' I said kindly, ''don't you see that just by thinking this way, you are helping that idea become our reality? You, yourself, are helping put the earth in its grave with your negative thinking,'' I added. I was trying to calm down, too, but it was hard. My grandmother's spirit was riding high inside of me. "Tell me, why is it that so many people are willing to believe in all the bad, in all the crap in the world, but they aren't willing to see the 99% that's good, that's healthy and wonderful? To see the miracle of each new day, the wonder of each new moment. Tell me, why is that? I don't understand. Why, we have an absolutely BEAUTIFUL WORLD! All we have to do is relax and, as the Navajos say, learn to walk within our own individual beauty."

"Jesus, you really do think that, don't you?" he said. "But then, tell me, what do you do when you see all this bad, disgusting evil in the world? What do you do?"

"I look at you, and I see good," I said, looking at him in the eyes. "I look at me, and I see good. I look around at all the world with my own two eyes and I see glorious blue sky and gorgeous green trees, birds and rocks, people and kids, and beautiful cars and tall, elegant buildings--like those buildings right over there, and each tree, each building, each person, each bird, each rock, is so beautiful, so gorgeous that I get hornier than hell, walking around all day wanting to--to, well, just to get it on with all the world and make passionate love with everything and everyone--cars, trees, buildings, people; oh, yes, particularly women from twenty-two to ninety-one; they're all so beautiful, and I'm so happy, so excited to feast my eyes on their beauty!" I smiled. "That's what I do," I added. ''Now, tell me, what do you do?''

''Well, I certainly don't do that,'' he said. He took a few deep breaths. ''No, truthfully, the evil I see in the world gets me down.''

''But why? Are you, yourself, so evil that you can't see the good in the world, too?''

He was taken aback. ''Well, no, not at all! Myself,'' he added, ''I'm a pretty good, decent guy...well, most of the time, anyway.''

''Well, then, why aren't you willing to give your fellow human beings and the world the same benefit of the doubt?''

Instantly, I could see he was frustrated again and getting angry. ''Because, well, of all I read and see--'' he began to tell me.

But I laughed. I wasn't angry anymore, and I cut him off. ''Sure, all you read on TV and see in the newspapers?''

He nodded. I laughed again, truly enjoying myself. He looked at me, really looked at me for the first time. ''You really are being straight with me, aren't you?'' he asked.

''Absolutely,'' I said.

''Then, you really do see peace, or at least 'lust' in the world when you look in the mirror in the morning?'' he said, laughing.

"Right!" I said, still laughing. "With all my heart and soul!"

He shook his head. "I don't get it. You look sane. I mean, to look at you, you don't look completely bonkers." He took a big breath. "I don't get it."

"Well, you see, I'm dyslexic," I said.

"Dyslexic?"

"Yes, that means that I could never quite learn to read very well. I could never get it. And the poor nuns," I added, laughing, "they even used to hit me on the head, trying to get it to sink into my skull, but I just kept asking more and more questions. So simply, my friend, I was never smart enough to get had. Were you a good student?"

"In college, I was. In high school I mostly played sports."

"Well, you see? I never did well in school at all."

"So, you're saying that going to school is a social handicap?"

"No, going to school isn't really a social handicap, but...much of 'classroom instruction' is pretty sick."

"Jesus! You really think that?"

"Sure. You see, when we're little kids, the whole world is full of magic. We can be anything or anyone and everything is possible! Particularly world peace. And I honestly do believe that my being dyslexic saved my ass from losing all that. That's how I managed to keep from being 'doped the rope', as my great hero Mohammed Ali so well said. God, I'd love to meet that man some day. He and Bob Dylan are my superheroes of the 20th Century! I'd just love to meet those two guys some day. I bet you money that they're both, maybe, a little bit dyslexic, too.''

"Do you have any women heroes?" he asked.

"Oh, sure, lots of them," I said. "But my favorites are Anne Frank, Eleanor Roosevelt, and Golden Manure. God, Golden is wonderful!''

"Golden Manure? Who's that?''

"You know that old woman from Israel, that tough, old Gandhi-type of woman.''

"Oh, you mean Golda Meir!'' He burst out laughing.

"You mean it's not 'Golden Manure'? Oh, I always kind of liked that. I thought her name stood for the true richness of the good earth.''

"MY GOD! YOU ARE SERIOUS!'' he screamed, he shouted, he stared at me, and burst out laughing.

"Sure, why not?" I said. "Dyslexia, that's the answer. You see, I got it audio as well as visual. I could just never get any of it straight when they started trying to brainwash me. I drove 'em crazy, the way I kept getting it all mixed up with having fun. I wasn't smart enough to catch on to what I was being taught. I flunked. I failed. I, I--'' I started laughing, too.

"Also, I'm sure that it helped me that I was never able to read a book until I was twenty. Because words, you know, all those little letters in a straight line, hurt my eyes and give me a headache. And you see, for the future to work, we're going to have to stop being so impressed with this little thing of ours called the 'brain' and allow kids to be kids until the age of seven or nine, at least.''

"You mean just let them run wild?''

"No, of course not. My two boys started doing chores at the age of three around the house and on our little ranch and even went to preschool. But it was a school that encouraged playing, singing, painting, and building things out of wood and clay. That encouraged, you know, creativity and getting dirty, and getting along with other kids down in the mud and fun of life. Not all that little uptight stuff of reading and writing and numbers and sitting up straight and keeping still. But big wild stuff with large playful strokes that encourages imagination and fun and loose-thinking and free-dreaming and doesn't hurt a dyslexic mind or destroys the wide-open wonderment that children naturally have for the universe!

"You see,'' I heard my grandmother telling me inside

my mind as I spoke, "each child that comes into the world is our latest messenger from God. Children aren't to be taught in their first seven years, but to be listened to and honored with love and understanding."

I could see that I had him now, he was now really listening. He wasn't fighting me anymore. We were now flowing together down the wide avenue of life and friendship and neighborhood. So I now told him about the "Snow Goose Vision" that I'd had, and that the time had come for the women and children to lead and for the men to step aside. The male's job was done, having "finished in beauty", and life from now on was to be enjoyed at a softer pace with love and *gusto* and mutual trust.

He started howling, really howling. "All right," he said, laughing, "so how does a person become dyslexic? I want to sign up!"

I laughed, too. "Great!" I said. "All you do to sign up is that we look into each other's eyes with *cariño*, affection, and shake hands." And I put out my hand once more and this time he took it. "Well, *amigo*," I said, looking at him in the eyes, "you and I have just become the first two official Snow Geese People For Global Thanksgiving And Peace And Harmony On Earth! Because, you see, you see me and you see good; I see you and I see good. And, no, we can't SOLVE all the problems of the world; there's just too many political, religious, and economical differences, but we sure as hell can DISSOLVE all the problems of the world by looking at each other in the eyes, one on one, and seeing that we are all God's children. Each and every one of us; we are all good people, and this is a wonderful, good earth, too!''

He smiled, pumping my hand. ''Hell, I'll shake on this all day long!''

And so we shook hands with power, with happiness, with love, and then he even let me give him an *abrazo*, a bear hug, right there on the street with people walking by us. I kissed him, and he didn't wipe it off or run away.

''Victor,'' I said.

''Jim,'' he said.

''Have a great day, Jim,'' I added. ''And a fabulous night.''

''You, too, Vic! See you. My God!'' he said, shaking his head. '''Golden Manure'!''

''Exactly, Jim,'' I said, ''Golden Manure, that's what we need; Golden Manure all over the earth so we can plant our miracle seeds of good tidings and watch our seeds grow into mighty trees! A whole forest all over the earth where the habit of peace and harmony can grow so strong that it will be hard to break for 5,000 years! Tell everyone, okay? Everybody!

We're wonderful and life is good!''

"Okay," he said, "I will. For sure. My God!" And he went up the street, smiling and shaking his head. He walked into a little Mexican take-out food place on the corner. He was still laughing, still smiling.

I pulled down my big western hat, being the real cowboy that I am, and I headed up the street to the Conant-Conant Book Store to tell the owners about the vision I'd had about cleaning up the "old plum tree" of all humankind and see if they could help me locate that big, handsome Indian who'd kicked my ass and got me started on this whole new wild adventure.

Damn, I felt TEN FEET TALL! And it was only daybreak; by sundown I was sure to have a couple of hundred Snow Goose People riding high on the spirit of peace and harmony on earth. Oh, I was raring to go! Grandmother was, indeed, right; this was the BIGGEST FUN ADVENTURE any person could have; PEACE AND HARMONY AND GOODWILL!

* * *

The bookstore wasn't open, and by 7:30 I was starving, so I stopped grabbing people off the street and panhandling them with peace and harmony for the next 5,0000 years---especially when a few of them took off in a quick hurry--and I went back to my hotel.

At 8 AM the owners of the Conant-Conant bookstore came by with their youngest son, and we had breakfast together in the hotel--damned good breakfast--and I told them all about my concept of Snow Goose Global Thanksgiving.

They loved it immediately, without hesitation, and they said that it would work, the time was right. People were so scared and desperate that they'd jump at anything that could bring them hope. Also, if it didn't work, for some unforeseen reason, then at least I still had planted the seeds of world peace and harmony in a lot of minds and so it would start making a difference as time went by. So it was a win-win-win proposition.

I thanked them and gave them each a hug and kiss, announcing that it was a beautiful day and we were all wonderful. Then they drove me to the airport along with their youngest son and I told them about the series of children's books that I had mapped out, like the one I'd worked on earlier this morning called *The Christmas Gift*. But I explained to them that these weren't really going to be children's books, but family books; books that parents would buy and read them WITH their children, so that they could then discuss the stories--I'd have a dozen questions at the end of each book--and together they could then relearn the "art" of tribal wisdom, which had no right or wrong answers but, instead, encouraged the simple joy of communicating as a family without the TV blasting.

Then I told them about the glorious vision that I'd had about us all being a tribe of Snow Geese, where the women and children led the way into the future and the males followed until danger was spotted, then they led for a short little while. And that the last 5,000 years had been that "little short while" of the males leading into the unknown valley of our modern age. But that it was now all over, having "finished in beauty", and now Our Grandfather Sky was coming back into "balance", with the Sun, the Moon, and Our Grandmother Earth.

They immediately got all excited about this too, and said it would work; yes, of course, and that they'd send me some children's books, so I could study them, and they wished me the ABSOLUTE BEST! I thanked them and spoke to their son, getting his ideas on the subject. And I found that he was still young enough to not worry about what society thought. He was still tapped into his own Guardian Angel Genius Of Himself that's inside each of us when we're kids and he gave me some brilliant ideas. I thanked him profusely.

At the airport they dropped me off, and I told them that

I'd keep them informed and that I was going to maybe take out an ad in the *L.A. Times* or the *New York Times*, a whole page, and announce to all the world that we, The Tribe Of The Snow Goose People, had arrived. I, also, said that I was going to go to Spain, to celebrate our first official Global Thanksgiving there, and invite the King and Queen to join us, so together we could start reversing the flow of all the negative energy that had been started with Columbus coming from Spain, and now we could begin an entirely-new life here on earth of love and goodwill among all humankind.

They loved it; they absolutely loved it, especially the Spain part, because then the whole process could begin where it had all originally got started off in the wrong step. I agreed, and we hugged and kissed with a big *abrazo*, and they said that they'd be ready to go to Spain with me on a week's notice! To please keep them informed!

Oh, I walked off feeling ten feet high! BOOKSTORE PEOPLE are the GREATEST PEOPLE in all the world, bar none! They're so open-hearted and well-informed and ready for new ideas! I waved goodbye to them, and then turned to the man who was checking in my bags at the curb. "Hello, friend, so what's your first reaction," I said, "to my saying that this upcoming Thanksgiving is the first official Global Thanksgiving of peace and harmony on earth for the next

5,000 years?''

He didn't answer me at first. He was large and very black, and he just kept working on my bags. I thought that maybe he hadn't heard me; but then he turned and looked at me and spoke in this deep, rich voice like a professional actor. He was gorgeous. ''Well, my first reaction is why this Thanksgiving?'' he said. ''Why not the last one? Last year was a really bad year around here.''

I was taken aback. ''You mean that's your reaction? You accept it? You just wish it would've started earlier?''

''Sure; why not?'' he said. ''Working around here, I hear a lot of crazy things every day, and the older I get, the more I'm beginning to like the crazy things I hear. It's those sane things, those self-righteous, important things that I hear that always seem to get us into the most problems in life. Sure, I accept what you say. Why not? It's about time!'' he added with a smile. ''It's about TIME!''

''Hey, I like that, *amigo mio*! The name is Victor.''

''Glad to meet you, Vic. I'm Jim.''

''Jim?''

''Yes, Jim.''

''Okay, Jim, you have now become the...let's see,'' I counted on my fingers, ''the fifth official Snow Goose of world peace on earth! Spread the word, Jim; this upcoming

Thanksgiving is the first official Global Thanksgiving of the next 5,000 years of peace and harmony on all the earth!''

"Sounds good to me, Vic, but man, you've got yourself a whole lot of telling to do between now and Thanksgiving.''

"No problem, Jim. You see, I'm--''

"Hey, weren't you written up in our Portland paper just the other day?'' he said, smiling grandly.

"Yes, I was,'' I said.

"Yeah, that's right, I read about you!''

"Good. Here, you want to read some more? I just happen to have about a dozen different reviews about my book, *Rain Of Gold*, on me. Here's the *U.S.A. Today, Sacramento Bee, N.Y. Times,* Denver, Chicago, *People* magazine, *L.A. Times, San Diego Tribune,* Washington DC--''

"Okay, okay, please, no more, Vic! This is plenty!''

"Just hold on; here is the Dallas one. I've got my big western hat on in this one. And here's *Publisher's Weekly,* you've got to read it first, because this article by Joe Barbato, my special angel, started the whole thing going for me. One man, one woman, one child can make all the difference in the world!''

"Okay, okay, please, no more, Vic!''

"All right, but now you've got to promise to read them

all and then pass them on to your friends. Here, give me your name and address on this card. Yeah, write it all down, and I'll be calling you and checking on you, so be sure that you read them and do your part for world peace, or I'll come back and give you more REVIEWS!''

"Okay, I will. I promise. Good God, it's still too early in the morning to be this fired up," he said.

"Bull! Bull! Bull!" I yelled. "It's going on nine, and I've been up since 2:30 AM, having visions and writing children's books for adults. IT'S LATE, Jim, I tell you, LATE! That's why we've got to KICK EVERYBODY'S ASS INTO PEACE AND HARMONY by this upcoming Thanksgiving--'cause it's almost getting TOO DAMN LATE, ALL OVER THE GLOBE!''

"Okay, okay, it's late. I agree. Boy, oh, boy! Glad to meet you, Vic. You're better than two cups of strong coffee!''

"Good! Here, give me a big *abrazo, amigo*." And so I hugged the big, black, handsome man, kissing him on each cheek, and then, "and, also, I want you to know that I'll be coming out with a little handbook for peace about Thanksgiving time. You'll be in the book, Jim, so be looking for it. And, the trick to Global Thanksgiving, Jim, is simple; all we got to do is relax and realize that we already got it. That's right, we already got peace and harmony on earth right now, at this very second as we're talking; for there have always been more good people on earth doing good things than scared, greedy little people doing "bad" things. See my point? So, all we got to do is open our eyes and realize this simple truth, we're good people already, you and me and everyone else, and concentrate our energies on the infinite goodness that's already here inside of us, and we're on our way! Up, up and away with the spirit of the Snow Goose! Have a good day, my friend," I added. "In fact, have a great day! You deserve it, Jim! Just look at you--old and healthy and gorgeous and, I bet, hornier than hell! You're a good man, Jim, and so am I!"

He was all grins. We hugged again, and then I was off, feeling so good and, once more, it hadn't cost a dime. Oh, this was good stuff, the greatest high in all the world, and it was free, FREE, FREE AND SO EASY!!!

I pulled down my big western hat and continued waltzing my way down the worldwide avenue of peace and harmony on earth, humming "Moon River, you old dream-maker, wider than a mile," and it was true! This was, indeed, the widest, fastest, safest avenue on the whole God-loving planet! And it was FUN! FUN! FUN! The biggest wild adventure around!

* * *

Getting on the plane, I was tired, so I just sat down in my seat and closed my eyes for a while. I felt the plane taxi down the runway, then take off. After we'd been airborne for some time, I opened my eyes and saw an elderly-looking businessman sitting by the window seat beside me and a youngish-looking woman in her thirties across the aisle from me. I decided to hit on the woman first.

"Tell me," I said to her, "what's the first thing that comes to your mind when I say that this upcoming Thanksgiving is our first official Global Thanksgiving and that we're now entering into 5,000 years of peace and harmony on earth?"

She was White and very well dressed. She looked at me, no doubt wishing that we weren't on a plane so she could just get the hell away from me. "Well, my first reaction is caution," she said nervously, jerking her head a little to the left. "I'm wondering what are you selling and how much is this going to cost me."

"What if I tell you that it's not going to cost a thing?" I said, sitting up. "In fact, here, you can have my money clip," I added, reaching in my Levis and taking out my money. "Take the whole thing, I don't care. It's about eighty dollars.''

She really didn't like what I was doing. "No, please," she said. "I don't want your money! Please, put it away!"

"Okay, then," I said, returning my money clip to my pocket, "what's your second reaction, Madam? What are you feeling, really feeling, when I say that the future of the world looks wonderful, in fact, is damn-right beautiful, and we're entering into a time of peace and harmony all over the globe?"

"Fear," she said.

"Fear?" I asked, completely taken aback.

"Yes," she said. "I feel fear, and then anger."

"Anger? But why fear and anger?" I asked, remembering how easily the big black man had accepted what I'd said. "What I'm saying is beautiful!"

"Because, well," she said, looking pretty upset, "I'd like to believe what you say, but I don't; and so it makes me ANGRY that you'd toy with me like THIS because by all indications--if you just read the papers and see what's going on--we're on the VERGE OF DISASTER!"

She was almost in tears. I took a deep breath. I could see that I'd really gone too far too quickly with her. My heart went out to her. Boy, like my grandmother had said, we really had gotten "lost" by telling each other of all these negative things about each other. "Look," I said, not wanting to lose her, "I'm not toying with you and I'm sorry if I came off sounding like that. But, you see, I had a vision last night...from my grandmother and I really do see how we can pull together all over the globe and slip into a world of peace and harmony for the next 5,000 years and...we can do it so easy." I smiled. "My name is Victor Villaseñor; I'm a writer. I wrote a book called *Rain Of Gold*. It's about both of my grandmothers coming from Mexico. It's a true story," I added and extended my hand.

"Glad to meet you," she said, taking my hand.

"Look," I said, "there's an old Mexican Indian saying that says that the reason that there's peace and harmony in the heavens is that all the heavenly bodies are female. That the only male is the sun, but he's such a coward of the darkness that they still don't let him out at night."

She laughed.

"Anyway," I continued, "that's what my book *Rain Of Gold* is about, it shows the power of the female, the power of my two grandmothers as they brought their families from Mexico to the United States at the turn of the century. You see, my grandmothers were these incredible, powerful women who never lost their faith in God or life, no matter what terrible disasters they had to live through. Rape, hunger, losing another child, war and destruction going on all around them, but still they gave thanks to God at the end of each day because they knew that that's the miracle of living, to realize that tomorrow is another day, another gift from God, and everything is going to turn out okay if we only keep our faith and keep going without getting bitter.''

I could see that she was calming down. ''And I'll tell you, my two grandmothers weren't that special or unusual; they were just your normal, average, poor Mexican Indian women, and now today, all over the earth we, also, have good, strong mothers busting their asses every hour of the day for their kids, just like my grandmothers, and a lot of them are single, but they still carry on with plenty of heart and love, making life good for their kids as best they can.

''So you see, what I'm saying is that the earth is a good place already, jam-packed with good people who are doing good deeds at this very moment, this very second, twenty-four hours a day! And that these good people and good deeds outnumber the negatives by 10,000 to one! Or, maybe, even 100,000 to one, but they just don't make the eleven o'clock news or the front page, and so we all tend to forget about these good deeds and good people. Am I making sense?''

''Well, yes, you are,'' she said. ''But I don't see what this has to do with world peace for 5,000 years.''

''Everything!'' I said. ''Don't you see, we already got

worldwide peace! All we have to do is stop listening to the 'bad' news, to all the crap that causes us to reinforce all the negative thinking that we have about ourselves, and start putting our energies into remembering what's good and wonderful about us.

"Truly, understand this simple fact, all of human history has been a stacked deck, a lie, an illusion, recorded by men who chose to think that wars and battles were the truth of history, that chose to think that violence is the basis of human nature, and it's not true. And our modern news has continued in that same negative war-like vein, perpetuating that same lie. But the truth is that there has always been more good people doing good things and living in peace and harmony on earth than there have been misguided power-hungry individuals causing war and destruction.

"War and violence was never the meat and potatoes of real life. Love has always been our basic power. Love, unconditional love, is what gave my grandmothers the heart, the nourishment, the soul to endure all the terrible things that happened to them. Love is what gave my dad, a little eleven-year-old boy, the strength to run all day and night through the desert without food or water and catch the train that his mother and sisters were on."

I stopped and took a good long look at her. "Think;

really think about this: What if history had been written by women all these years, by mothers, by grandmothers? Hell, I'll tell you, we'd be living in a totally different reality. What we think is human, human nature, would be very, very different. Do you see what I mean? The time in human history has come for us to turn off our TVs and stop listening to the "bad" news and go back to basics, to visiting with our neighbors, our loved ones, and "rediscover" how wonderful we really are! To 'discover' what Columbus never 'discovered'--and that is that you don't find lasting happiness or economical salvation by crossing oceans and abusing other people, but by staying home and recreating yourself and realizing that we have a pretty damn good, wonderful world already.

"And I don't mean for us to forget history or just close our eyes! No, I mean for us to open our eyes big, REALLY BIG, and learn from history, but by recounting all of history honestly; by putting into our history books not just stories about Hitler and Columbus and all these other misguided men and women; but, by also putting into our history books all of these other people--good people--who were living at the same time as Hitler and Columbus, and who were living good, normal, productive lives, but they never made it into the history books. And these people, the vast majority of humankind, are the real heroes of life!

"Do you see what I mean, we, the meek, the nobodies, aren't going to inherit the earth some day. Hell, no! We inherited the earth long ago! And now all we got to do is OPEN OUR EYES BIG and see this WONDERFUL TRUTH!"

I didn't mean to, but I began to cry. "My grandmothers, these poor, uneducated nobodies, they are the real power of the earth! They really are, and they have always been the real power, but they were never given their rightful credit." I dried my eyes. "Oh, please, understand me, incomplete histories distort life, and it hurts! Honestly, you can't imagine how awful it was for me to grow up in this country and think that I was no good, I was a nobody; that Mexicans ARE the enemy, the 'bad guys' in all cowboy movies and that my grandmothers were, were nothing but poor, dirty nobodies!"

I stopped, I swallowed, and wiped my eyes. "Please, tell me, am I making any sense?" I asked the woman. "Does any of this come across? Because, I swear, we really are good people, all of us, we really are, and the earth is good, too."

"Well," she said, taking a large breath, "I can now see that you really do mean what you say and that this idea of world peace and harmony is important to you, personally, but I still can't see how one person's feelings--no matter how well intended--can reach the whole world."

I looked at her. I really looked at her, and took a big breath and realized that she had really heard me and that she was now being absolutely real with me. I closed my eyes. I closed my eyes and I could feel the power of the huge jet under us as we flew over the earth's surface. I kept my eyes closed and I asked my grandmother to help me, to give me the wisdom to answer this woman her question. I breathed. I breathed, and then I felt a peace, a light-good-feeling come into me, and I smiled and opened my eyes.

"Look at me," I said, smiling.

She did as I requested.

"You see, when two people look at each other, really look at each other in the eyes and forget the whole rest of the world, then there's a little bit of magic, a little bit of peace, created on earth." I smiled again. "Do you feel a little of this peace, of this magic, right now?"

She nodded. "Yes. I do, a little."

I smiled. "Me, too! So you see, that's the key to all of world peace. For people to simply start taking the time to look at one another in the eyes, the mirror of our souls, and say 'Hi. Hello, friend!' And that's it." I breathed. "And then for three hours once a year--on Thanksgiving Day--for all of us all over the land to take the time to look into each other's eyes and forget all the world, all our problems, and forgive all of our trespasses that we've done or think that we've done to each other, and say 'Hi. Hello!' to our loved ones, and give thanks for all of the good things that we already have and the whole world will rejoice." I smiled. "Can you do that? Once a year for just three hours."

"Well, yes, of course," she said, "I can do that, but what you must understand is that there are a lot of people out there who are so--"

"Please," I said, closing my eyes. "Please don't concern yourself about others. Forget the world. Just forget the world and all the 'others' and take care of yourself. Please, just yourself." I opened my eyes. "Can you do that, forget all the 'others', and just take care of yourself, *numero uno*, once a year for three hours?"

She looked at me, and it was difficult for her, really difficult, but finally she said, "Yes, I can do that."

I smiled. "Good. Wonderful. Then, that's all that's needed." I started to laugh. I could feel my grandmother radiating through me. "You see, we really don't need to do that much to have world peace, all we got to do is for you and me, each one of us, to aim one little tiny centimeter higher than we normally aim in our daily lives and shoot our energy around the globe and when that energy comes back to us again--having circled the earth--we'll be flying! WE'LL ALL BE

FLYING five miles above the earth's surface just as we are now doing inside of this airplane and we'll be riding on THE WINGS OF ANGELS!

"For, you see, every person that I've asked so far tells me that yes, of course, they can do it; it's only them, the others, who can't. But you see, there are no 'them', there are no 'others', there are no 'enemies', there are no 'bad' people. There's only us, me and you, all over the globe, and we're 'good' people. In fact, you and I are wonderful! For we are Snow Goose Angels!"

I laughed again and my eyes began to water freely and I took this youngish-woman's hand in both of my hands and I now told her about the "Snow Goose Vision" that I'd had, and about my grandmother, and about the big handsome Indian who'd pushed me, and how "History" was coming to a close, having "finished in beauty", and now we were entering "Herstory" and the Snow Geese were showing us the way and that this was no fly-by-night idea, because the Snow Geese had been living in peace and harmony for over two million years and so this upcoming Thanksgiving was going to be, indeed, wonderful! Our first official giant baby-step into the next 5,000 years of our own peace and harmony, and it was going to be so easy! So very easy!

"Believe me, the aggressive, tough men of the world

had their chance for the last 10,000 years,'' I said to her, ''and they haven't brought us any closer to peace and harmony, or wisdom and happiness, and so it's time to fire their asses and try something new. Hell, I'm beginning to finally understand that it was never these males' intent to ever deliver peace or harmony to us. No, it was always their intent, whether they consciously knew it or not, to keep the world ''off balance'' with fear and war and tales of eternal damnation, so they could keep the control of things and out of the hands of the women and children! So I say, let's fire their asses and start anew, right now!''

Her whole face lit up. ''With this, I fully agree!'' she said. ''It is time to do something new! My God, there are so many incompetent men where I work that it boggles the mind!''

''You said it,'' said the woman in front of us, turning around in her seat. ''In my company, too! Men are spoiled! They've had it too easy! And I'd like you to know--'' she said, glancing at me,''--that I can honestly agree with many of the things you said, but I, also, emphatically disagree with many of the things you stated.''

''Thank God!'' I said, laughing. ''I'd hate to meet the person who agreed with me on everything! Why, they'd be totally bonkers!''

The two women laughed and started talking together, forgetting all about me, which I loved. Because, for all this to work on a global level, people were going to have to take off and fly on their own Snow Goose wings.

I took off my western hat, put it on the seat next to me, and snuggled down tight in my seat so I could take a little nap as we flew down to the Bay Area. But then I noticed that the older-looking businessman who was sitting by the window seat next to me looked pretty pensive. I wondered if he'd been intimidated by my words. I had said some pretty rough things about men. "Excuse me," I said to him, "but I see that you look kind of quiet. How do you feel about what I just said? Are you upset about my saying it's time for men to step aside and let the women and children lead or they should get their asses fired?"

He turned and stared at me, really stared at me. He was in his late sixties and looked very successful, but truly tired. His eyes were puffy and the skin on his face sagged with worry. He glanced over at the two women who were still talking excitedly. "No, I'm not upset, son," he said quietly. "I just got married again for the third time, not too long ago, and...I was thinking, you know, that maybe, well, I've been the problem all along, always trying to make another buck instead of being home more often with the kids and my wife." He took a few deep breaths, never taking his eyes off of me. "No," he said, reaching out and putting his hand on my shoulder. "I'm not upset with what you said, son; in fact, I like what you said and I only wish that I'd maybe heard you twenty years ago."

He smiled, and his whole face came away from that mask that he was used to wearing. I could feel a warmth coming from his hand on my shoulder.

"You know," he said, "I think I'm going to maybe fire my own ass as soon as I get home and relax for awhile. I'm tired, really tired; and, sure, let the women take the lead for awhile. Fine with me. I need the rest, God knows."

"You're a good man," I said, feeling all this warmth and love coming from him. "The best."

"You wouldn't say that if you knew me, son."

"Oh, yes, I would," I said.

He breathed. "No, son," he said very seriously. "I've crushed a lot of people in my day."

"So," I said, breathing deeply, too, and keeping a tight hold on the love that I was feeling for him. I wasn't going to let myself get sidetracked with a bunch of high-sounding principles and judgments. No, I was going to keep looking at him in the eyes, one on one, and remember that we were all children of God. "Did you crush more people than Hitler?"

I asked. "Did you cause more slaughter than Columbus has caused in the last 500 years?"

"Well, no, of course not," he said.

"Well, then, you're a good man!" I said. "Because, you see, the truth is that even Hitler and Columbus were good men, too. Take Hitler, for instance; do you realize that he would have gone down in history as one of the greatest statesman of the world, if he'd quit in his first five years. You see, what makes men usually bad, or maybe even most of the time, is that they don't quit in time. They start taking themselves too seriously and start listening to all these cowardly hang-oners who are too chicken-shit to go out and do it themselves.

"So, no, you're a good man and so was Columbus. Now all you got to do is go home and fire your ass and start using all that power that you've used to make money, to now start helping clean up this old world and to bring peace and harmony between all us human beings. And, remember, *amigo*, you start with your own family; you start with them right now, as soon as you get home, and I say to you that you are a good man! In fact, a wonderful man; no two ways about it! And I don't care how much an asshole you've been in the past! You're my good *amigo* now, and I want a hug, an *abrazo*, and right now! *Amigo mio!*"

His eyes, that mask of death that he was accustomed to wearing, cracked just a little, and then fell apart into quick pieces, and now those puffy eyes and that saggy chin began to soften up before my very eyes. It was a miracle. I reached out and I took him in my arms and I held him close, giving him all the love of the universe that came flowing through me UNCONDITIONALLY. And this big, old, powerful bulldog of a man in his late sixties held onto me like he hadn't been hugged in twenty thousand years. I mean, he gave me such a wonderful *abrazo* of hunger, of naked open-heart that it brought tears to my eyes and then I saw that he was crying, too. I kissed him, then kissed him again, and then I realized that people were watching us. In fact, the two women were staring at us in astonishment.

"Hello," I said to the first woman I'd spoken to. "I'd like you to meet my friend...what's your name?"

"Jim," said the older man.

"This is my friend, Jim," I said. "And he's agreed to fire his own ass when he gets home and spend more time with his loved ones."

The second woman, the one who was turned about in her seat, had tears in her eyes. "I'm Jane," she said, "glad to meet you, Jim. And you," she said to me, "I'd like you to know that you are wonderful."

"Yes, I am," I said, smiling. "I am wonderful. And you are wonderful, too. Because it takes a wonderful person to accept another person's wonderfulness."

She laughed, drying her eyes. "I'm going to buy your book, *Rain Of Gold*," she said, "the moment we get off the plane. Do you do house calls, too?"

I laughed. "No. I'm a writer. That's my job, and I do appreciate you buying my book, and you'll love it. It's a great book."

"I'm sure it is," she said.

"I'm buying one, too," said the other woman.

"Good. Or buy a dozen! They make great Christmas gifts."

Jim laughed.

"What's so funny?" I asked.

"Oh, nothing."

"Come on, it was something."

"Well," he said, "I was just about to say that it's probably just cheaper to give you twenty bucks than to buy all those books." He grinned. "But I caught myself." He laughed. "Old habits are hard to break." Jim laughed again. He looked ten years younger. "Women leading, how about that?"

"And children, too," I added. "Remember, they're

our latest messengers from God and we got to start listening
to them--'' I touched my chest. ''--with our hearts.''

* * *

I closed my eyes for the remainder of the flight and
slept like a baby. The Sky opened up and here were all these
Snow Goose People with great huge white wings and there
was a huge banquet of food on long tables, stretched up and
down the length of this colorful little neighborhood. And the
people kept streaming out of their homes, carrying platters of
food and drums of drink and the Sun smiled and the Earth
rejoiced and everyone was laughing and talking and eating and
then I, suddenly, realized what was at the very center, at the
very core of Global Thanksgiving; why, simply, it was food.
Lots and lots of food and love; where all hearts opened and all
wines flowed.

I slept and continued dreaming and the people came
out of their homes and I saw that yes, indeed, the time had
come for all of God's children from all over the globe to join
together in a great feast. A great feast of different foods and
religions and customs and beliefs and clothes and colors and
music and languages; where all hearts opened with unconditional love and all wines flowed free of any judgments. And

at each table I saw Indians and Pilgrims, Chinese and Mexicans, Africans and Indonesians, Hawaiians and Eskimos, and some brought food and drink, others brought hunger and thirst, and it was glorious. Simply glorious, and then out of the crowd I saw my father stand up and say, "Eat and be merry! And if you want to join us in our celebration of Global Thanksgiving, good! But if you don't, that's okay, too! Because we're going to feed you anyway!" And he laughed and laughed. "In fact," he added, "we're going to keep feeding you every year from now on! Because nobody, but nobody is going to be allowed to get off this old world anymore without being fed and loved at least one day a year!"

People loved it and started applauding and my dad drank down his tequila and started dancing. I laughed and continued sleeping, dreaming, and the Sun went down and the Moon came up and all the Heavens rejoiced. And I then saw that this was, indeed, not a dream, but a true happening, and it was happening right now, today, on Judgment Day. The Day on which all human beings finally realized that we are, indeed, all children of God, and we no longer passed judgment on one another, for God loved us no matter what, and so now we could all relax, too, and love each other no matter what. Amen! Awomen! Achildren!

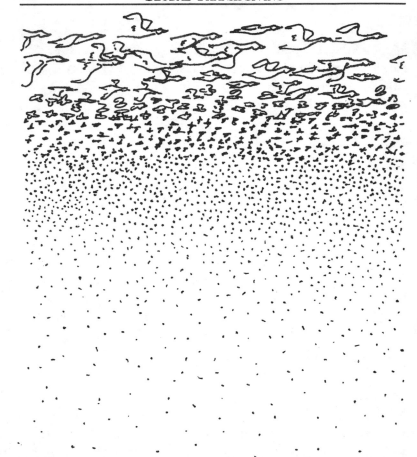

Three Hundred Thousand Snow Geese Flying East
By David Cuauhtemoc Villaseñor

SO, DID SPAIN REALLY HAPPEN?

Of course Spain really happened. Did you ever have any doubt? I took out a whole page ad in our local Oceanside newspaper--they actually ended up giving me the whole page almost free--writing a crazy wild story about my ''Snow Goose Vision'' and ''Columbus' three lost little white ships'' and invited all the world to join us. We received hundreds of wonderful letters and dozens of pictures of grade-school kids making ''Snow Goose Outfits'' and celebrating Global Thanksgiving, and then forty-two of us flew to Spain. We have 9½ hours of film of our trip, and right now we're in the process of reducing those 9½ hours to a twenty-minute film so we can show it to people.

This year, 1993, I'm going to I'll take out another ad, using part of this text, and we're going to Plymouth Rock, and then the following year, we've been invited to go to Costa Rica and join forces with the people from University of Peace in Costa Rica.

The word is spreading, and it's beautiful! And people are coming with power, with energy, and they're inexhaustible with their love just like my grandmother said that they would be. *Gracias*! Thank you! Let us all walk in God's Beauty!

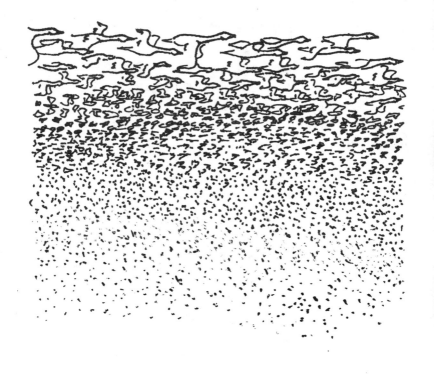

Six Hundred Thousand Snow Geese Flying East
By David Cuauhtemoc Villaseñor

WHAT COULD BE THE DOWNSIDE TO ALL THIS?

Nothing. There is no downside to this. There is only up, up and away, into a glorious world of peace and harmony and goodwill among all humankind.

You see, take care of yourself and the world will take care of itself. Make yourself happy, and the world will be happy. That's it. Nothing more and nothing less. That simple. All reality is our-own-self-mirror, thank God.

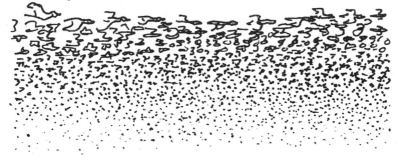

Seven Hundred Thousand Snow Geese Flying East
BY DAVID CUAUHTEMOC VILLASEÑOR

ARE THERE ANY HIDDEN AGENDA?

No. There are no hidden agenda. What you see is what you get; crazy, happy, full of *gusto*, God-loving worldwide peace and harmony for the next 5,000 years!

Nine Hundred Thousand Snow Geese Flying East
By David Cuauhtemoc Villaseñor

AS A JEW, CHRISTIAN, MUSLIM, OR BUDDHIST OR WHATEVER, AM I BEING ASKED TO COMPROMISE MY FAITH IN ANY WAY WHATSOEVER?

Absolutely not. Enjoy your faith. Truly, enjoy it. For we all need our OWN faith. And, if any word in this rapbook offends you after you've read the book in its entirety three or four times, then cross it out and only keep what you like. Because easy does it. After all, we're all children of God, and so let us not be separated by our little differences, but UNITED BY OUR MUCH, MUCH LARGER UNCONDITIONAL LOVE OF GOD!

Nine Million Snow Geese Flying East
By David Cuauhtemoc Villaseñor

OKAY, I'M IN...NOW WHAT?

Continue being happy. That's it; just continue being happy and forgiving our trespasses and let's get together once a year. And by the year 2026, we'll be a billion strong, and the whole rest of the world will be listening, and we'll have it made; our first giant baby step into the next 5,000 years of peace and harmony on earth will be complete. Because with this many Snow Goose People, the entire axis of the world will turn and be in our hands, and everywhere people will find themselves smiling, laughing, being happy, and they won't even know why.

Remember, where reason DARE NOT GO!

Ninety Million Snow Geese Flying East
By David Cuauhtemoc Villaseñor

BUT HOW DO WE KNOW IF WE'RE ON THE RIGHT PATH?

Easy. Just listen to your heart and relax, really relax down deep inside, and let the light shine through that's already here inside you. Be a child again and glow in the magic that's all around us. Enjoy. And let's have fun cleaning up the old plum tree. Lots and lots of FUN!!!

Three Hundred Million Snow Geese Flying East
By David Cuauhtemoc Villaseñor

ARE WE OPEN TO SUGGESTIONS, TO INFORMATION, OR COMMENTS?

Absolutely. Please, write and send them to us. We need all the help we can get. Plus, that way, we'll have your address and we can keep you informed on what we'll be doing. And don't worry; we're not going to ever ask you for any money. Not one single dime. World peace and harmony are FREE! For they come straight from the heart!

Six Hundred Million Snow Geese Flying East
By David Cuauhtemoc Villaseñor

ALL RIGHT, I'M REALLY IN, BUT CAN WE AS HUMAN BEINGS TRULY EVER FORGIVE A HITLER OR A COLUMBUS, OR A FATHER OR FRIEND WHO RAPED US, WHO HURT US, WHO DESTROYED US?

Well, *amigo, amiga,* this is the biggie, the real biggie; for if we can't forgive, truly forgive, and go on with our lives, then we're sunk. Because when we don't forgive, then what we are doing is carrying that "wrong", that "pain", that "terrible thing" that happened to us here inside of our heart, and we're giving it life, thought, nourishment, and we're not only destroying ourselves with it, but we're, also, adding to all the poison, all the negativity that's already in the world. And the "bad guys" won.

Because, I'll tell you, that person or group who did the "wrong" or caused the "pain" has probably forgotten all about you, or has turned the whole thing all around inside their head and put the blame on you, and they've gone on with their lives and are quite happy.

Look at the old Nazis that they keep digging up. Most of them are in good health and look pretty good.

So the best revenge of all is to just drop "it", to refuse to carry that "pain" or "hurt" or want of revenge. To just quit feeding any anger or bad feelings to that experience anymore and just go on with your life and live a good, happy life. That's how you really "get even" with the "bad guys" who've done you wrong or caused you pain, is to forget them, forgive them, and just chalk it up as an experience, as a challenge, as a chance to grow bigger, WAY BIGGER, and live a good, happy life!

Like my own dad, he hated Tom Mix, the movie star, with a passion because his no-good racist movies caused a lot of problems in the barrio. And so when my dad got rich, what did he do? Why, he hired somebody to find out how big Tom Mix's house was in Hollywood, and then my dad built a bigger house. Twenty-two rooms right near the ocean in Oceanside, overlooking our own private inlet of water. This is the best revenge of all, my dad always said; screw them, and just enjoy your life! Give 'em no satisfaction whatsoever! And live a good, happy life!

Like look at all the teachers who used to call me "stupid" and hit me on the head; now they have to read my books, watch me on TV and see my name in all the papers and when they run into me on the street in my home town, they try and befriend me. And you know, to my happy surprise, I treat them well. Because, you see, they don't own me; I own me! For I forgave them long ago, and that's my power; I earned myself! The buck stops here! I took that pain, that wrong they did to me, and I blossomed with it! Ha, ha, ha! Ha, ha, ha! I WON! And the more crap life gives me, the more I'll KEEP GROWING! So love your enemy, no kidding, for they caused you to become the great wonderful person that you are!

And, please don't think I'm making light of your situation if you've been beaten or raped or forced to see your kids killed in front of you by drugs or gangs or cops or armies, or sadistic sick people, because I'm not. My grandmother, Doña Margarita, had nineteen children and fourteen lived to adulthood and within four years of the Mexican Revolution, she only had three left. Three--that's all! But she never gave up or became bitter. No, each night she'd kneel down with her family and give thanks to God, for tomorrow was another day. So go in peace, my friend. Remember, God loves you, no matter what!

Seven Hundred Million Snow Geese Flying East
By David Cuauhtemoc Villaseñor

ARE WE A SUCCESS?

Yes, of course we're a success! Was there was ever any doubt? Because when you are wonderful, then the whole world is wonderful, too.

Keep the faith! *Con Dios!* Walk in Beauty, my friend!

Nine Hundred Million Snow Geese Flying East
By David Cuauhtemoc Villaseñor

ARE WE HAPPY?

Yes!

One Billion Snow Geese Are Now Preparing To Land, As Three Big Males Drop Out Of The Tribe; Chests Open, Hearts True, Dropping, Dropping In ALL Their Grace And Elegance

THE SONG OF THE SNOW GEESE

I went to bed dreaming
Of the troubles in the land
When I was awakened by such commotion
I could not understand
I went to the window
And much to my surprise
I saw three wondrous, big white birds
Coming from the sky...singing

    Wee, wee, wee in peace and understanding
    Wee, wee, wee sing of love and harmony
    Wee, wee, wee like the sound of children laughing
    Wee, wee, wee came the song from the Snow Geese

The sight was so amazing
I went outside to see more
And by the time I reached my front porch
There were nine or ten birds more
A gaggle of them, giggling and flying around
All singing the same song
I blinked twice and before my eyes
Twenty more had joined the throng...singing

    Wee, wee, wee in peace and understanding
    Wee, wee, wee sing of love and harmony
    Wee, wee, wee like the sound of children laughing
    Wee, wee, wee came the song from the Snow Geese

Suddenly a sadness
Welled up inside of me
I wanted to join in the song
But didn't know how that could be
So I cried out to the big white birds
I've no wings to soar with you
Then in unison they spoke back to me
Said all you gotta do...is sing,

 Wee, wee, wee in peace and understanding
 Wee, wee, wee sing of love and harmony
 Wee, wee, wee like the sound of children laughing
 Wee, wee, wee came the song from the Snow Geese

Well since that night I, too, fly
High above the ground
Singing a song of peace and love
To people all around
And like the birds of purest white
I'll take this song to all who'll hear
Peace is just around the corner
It's the new frontier...let's sing,

 Wee, wee, wee in peace and understanding
 Wee, wee, wee sing of love and harmony
 Wee, wee, wee like the sound of children laughing
 Wee, wee, wee came the song from the Snow Geese

 Wee, wee, wee, wee, wee, wee, wee

Remember, 100% of all profits go into the perpetuation of the Global Thanksgiving non-profit organization.

To order more copies of this Snow Goose Global Thanksgiving publication, complete the order form on the next page. Price is $9.95 each. Please add postage/handling as follows: $1.50 for the first book and 50 cents for each additional book (this price is for U.S. only).

Send check or money order (no C.O.D.s, please) to:

RANCHO VILLASEÑOR
1302 Stewart Street
Oceanside, CA 92054

Please allow one to two weeks for delivery.

I have enclosed $_____ for _____ copies of Snow Goose Global Thanksgiving (which includes the appropriate postage and handling).

Please mail to:

_____
Name

_____
Address

_____
City, State   Zip Code

I have enclosed $_____ for _____ copies of Snow Goose Global Thanksgiving (which includes the appropriate postage and handling).

Please mail to:

_____
Name

_____
Address

_____
City, State   Zip Code